THE CHRISTIAN MANHOOD PLEDGE

THE CHRISTIAN MANHOOD PLEDGE

Study Guide

MICHAEL D. MAUNEY

The Christian Manhood Pledge
Michael D. Mauney
Copyright © 2024 Michael Dean Mauney
All rights reserved.
ISBN: 979-8-218-52827-0

The publisher prohibits the reproduction, distribution, or transmission of any part of this book, in any form or by any means—through photocopying, recording, or other electronic or mechanical methods—without prior written permission. Exceptions are made only for brief quotations used in critical reviews and specific noncommercial purposes as copyright law permits. For permission requests, please contact the publisher by writing to 'Attention: Permissions Coordinator' at the email below.

Editing and Assistance
The author edited this book with the assistance of Grammarly and ChatGPT. ChatGPT also contributed to creating the artwork and images in this book.

Scripture Quotations
The author used Scripture quotations from the ESV® Bible (The Holy Bible, English Standard Version®), copyright © 2001 by Crossway, a Good News Publishers publishing ministry, with permission. All rights reserved.

Disclaimer
This book is a work of nonfiction. The author has made every effort to ensure the information is accurate as of the publication date. However, the author disclaims any liability for any loss, damage, or disruption caused by errors or omissions resulting from negligence, accident, or any other cause.

Publisher Information
Published by TMI Publishing
Distributed by Amazon KDP
Printed in the United States of America
First Edition

For permission requests or other inquiries, please contact:
contact@themanhoodinstitute.com

PRESENTED TO | THIS BOOK BELONGS TO

_____

_____

BY | PURCHASED BY

_____

_____

DATE

_____

"Be strong and courageous. Do not be frightened, and do not be dismayed, for the Lord your God is with you wherever you go."
— Joshua 1:9

DEDICATION

I lovingly dedicate this book to my sons, **Caleb** and **Donovan**. God Almighty entrusted me with the privilege of being your father, and as our Heavenly Father said of His Son, I am well pleased with you both. You are my greatest blessings, and I pray that you continue to walk in the purpose and strength that God has placed upon your lives.

I also dedicate this book to all men so that you may seek a deeper relationship with God and embrace the journey of faith. May you rise to the call of Christian manhood, living a life that reflects God's love, grace, and commitment to His people.

ACKNOWLEDGMENTS

First and foremost, I thank God for entrusting me with The Christian Manhood Pledge's vision and guiding me in writing this book. This journey would not have been possible without His grace, wisdom, and strength.

I want to thank Pastor Anthony Moore and the brothers of The Man Cave at Carolina Missionary Baptist Church for their encouragement, brotherhood, and spiritual support throughout this process. Your fellowship and insights have been invaluable in shaping this work.

To my coworkers, thank you for your thoughtful feedback on this book. Your insights and suggestions have helped refine and enhance the message I aim to share, and for that, I am genuinely grateful.

I thank Dr. Harold Bennett for his guidance and contributions and Jimmy West for his invaluable editorial assistance. Your keen eye and thoughtful input were essential in completing this book.

To my sons, Caleb and Donovan, thank you for your love, inspiration, and unwavering support. You have been a source of strength, and I am forever grateful for your role in helping me complete this book.

I always tell my friends that if friendship were measured in money, I would be the richest man in the world. Thank you for your companionship and encouragement—a special thanks to the brothers of Kappa Alpha Psi for your guidance in achievement. To my friends in the Tuesday and Thursday night prayer circle, your unwavering support and prayers have been a constant source of strength and inspiration. I am deeply grateful to each of you.

I thank Dr. Diane Mosby, Dr. Sabrina St. Clair, and Dr. Harold Bennett. Since we met at STVU, you have fostered a deep and lasting relationship built on mutual trust, respect, and care—emotionally and spiritually. I am forever grateful for your support and friendship.

Lastly, I would also like to recognize my family. To my mother, Pauline Mauney, and sister, Sheila McCain—thank you for everything you have done for me—much love to my aunts, uncles, cousins, nieces, and nephews for your constant support.

Family is the foundation upon which we build our lives. Through their love and support, we learn resilience, loyalty, and strength from standing together. My family has always been my anchor, reminding me I am never alone. Our shared history and bond have shaped me into who I am today, and I am forever grateful for that.

CONTENTS

FORWARD XI

PREFACE XIII

INTRODUCTION HOW TO USE THIS BOOK 1

CHAPTER 01. LOVE AND DEVOTION 13

CHAPTER 02. DILIGENCE AND PROSPERITY 25

CHAPTER 03. PROTECTION AND LOVE 37

CHAPTER 04. DEFENDER OF CHILDHOOD 47

CHAPTER 05. HONORING AND UPLIFTING WOMEN 59

CHAPTER 06. HEALTH AND PURITY 69

CHAPTER 07. COMMUNITY SUPPORT AND UNITY 85

CHAPTER 08. DIVINE STRENGTH AND GUIDANCE 97

CHAPTER 09. FINAL STEP 119

APPENDICES 125

ABOUT THE AUTHOR 137

EMPOWERING THROUGH EDUCATION AND TRAINING 138

FORWARD

Foreword by Dr. Harold Bennett

I first met Michael Mauney in 2001 at the C. Rodger Wilson Leadership Conference of Kappa Alpha Psi in Williamsburg, VA. What began as a simple request for a ride back to Maryland became pivotal. Before leaving the parking lot, Michael asked if he could pray for our safe travels. During that prayer, Michael boldly declared that God was calling me into ministry. Initially, I thought he was joking, but his sincerity and conviction left a lasting impression.

For months after that, Michael persistently encouraged me to pursue seminary, believing it was part of God's assignment for him. His encouragement was more than a suggestion—it was spiritual accountability, a quality that has defined Michael's ministry and leadership. We eventually attended the Samuel DeWitt Proctor School of Theology at Virginia Union University together. From the beginning, it was clear that Michael was committed to bringing others along in their spiritual journey.

Michael's heart for helping men grow in their faith has been unwavering throughout the years. He has always focused on empowering men to live with purpose, integrity, and spiritual discipline. This vision is at the core of *The Christian Manhood Pledge*.

This book is a powerful guide for men committed to aligning their lives with God's will. Michael challenges us to confront our thoughts, behaviors, and actions, ensuring our faith remains steadfast. As men, we often face pressures that can shake our foundation. Still, Michael reminds us that true strength lies in our spiritual stability. When we are rooted in faith, we can weather any storm.

One of Michael's greatest legacies is his role as a father. His commitment to raising his sons in the faith reflects the Biblical call to fatherhood in **Genesis 18:19**: *"For I have chosen him, that he may command his children and his household after him to* *keep the way of the Lord by doing righteousness and justice."* Michael's sons, Caleb and Donovan, are walking testimonies of this commitment, following their father's path before them.

The Christian Manhood Pledge is more than a book—it's a manual for men seeking to grow closer to God, lead with integrity, and remain firm in their faith. Michael's journey and ministry serve as a powerful example; through this book, he invites all men to walk this path with him.

Dr. Harold Bennett, D.Min.
Pastor, Grove Presbyterian Church

PREFACE

The concept for this book study was born out of a personal experience during our church's Father's Day program at Carolina Missionary Baptist Church in Fort Washington, Maryland, under the inspiring leadership of Senior Pastor Anthony Moore. To honor and challenge the men in our congregation, I initially developed a set of eight pledges, each carefully crafted with four meaningful sentences to encapsulate the essence of Christian manhood. However, due to the time constraints of the program, I condensed these pledges to two sentences each, ensuring they remained impactful while fitting in with the time we had available.

The response from the congregation was overwhelmingly positive, with many men expressing a desire for a more detailed and robust framework to help them live out these pledges in their daily lives. When I later shared the pledge with some of my co-workers, they echoed this feedback and expressed their need for guidance in carrying out these commitments in their own lives. It became clear that the message and purpose of these pledges resonated beyond the church, touching the hearts of men from various walks of life who were seeking direction and support in their spiritual journeys.

Inspired by this widespread interest and the call for a more comprehensive resource, I decided to expand upon the original concept of the pledge in this book. By doing so, I aim to provide a deeper understanding and more thorough guidance for men committed to embodying the principles of *The Christian Manhood Pledge*.

Each chapter in this book starts with a pledge that focuses on essential themes of Christian manhood. These pledges are made stronger by a carefully chosen quote that sets the tone for the chapter. The pledge and the quote encourage readers to think deeply, offering a starting point for personal reflection and growth.

As you work through each chapter, you will find thoughtful exploration that illuminates the significance of the pledge, along with practical insights to help you apply these principles in your everyday life. Each chapter concludes with tailored exercises to promote self-reflection and personal action, supporting the reader's journey. While some exercises may seem directed toward those who are married or fathers, each activity remains relevant to all men, regardless of life stage or relationship status. These exercises challenge you to move from understanding to practice, ensuring the lessons become integral to your spiritual walk and personal growth.

I have included the complete Christian Manhood Pledge at the end of this introductory chapter to reinforce these themes. This comprehensive pledge summarizes the commitments found throughout the book. It is a guide to inspire and direct your spiritual journey. Each pledge, quote, and exercise contributes to a holistic approach that encourages knowledge and transformation—helping you integrate these values into every aspect of your life and remain steadfast in your faith.

In addition, I have provided a **Pre-Evaluation and Post-Evaluation** table for each pledge, designed to help you measure your growth in these critical areas. This self-assessment allows you to reflect on your progress as you build upon your strengths and develop the areas where you may struggle. By revisiting the evaluation at the end of your journey, you'll gain deeper insights into your transformation and growth as you strive to live out these pledges.

The Christian Manhood Pledge encourages men to thoroughly live out Christian characteristics connected to manhood. This multifaceted commitment highlights the importance of spiritual, moral, mental, social, political, and economic advancement by drawing on biblical concepts to encourage men daily. The pledge calls for men to live out their faith in practical and impactful ways by loving their neighbors as themselves, engaging in diligent enterprise, protecting and cherishing their families, respecting women, safeguarding children, and maintaining personal health and well-being. The Christian Manhood Pledge also encourages men to strengthen their relationship with God, seeking His guidance and support in every aspect of their lives. It aims to inspire men to lead by example, fostering positive change within their families, communities, and beyond while deepening their spiritual connection and reliance on divine strength in all their endeavors.

Preface

About the Book Cover

This book's cover thoughtfully encapsulates its message, inspiring men to embody the principles of Christian manhood in every aspect of their lives. The cover features carefully chosen elements representing the intersection of faith, commitment, and community in various facets of life.

At the center, two men shake hands with a cross, symbolizing the covenant of faith and brotherhood foundational to the Christian journey. Surrounding this central image are rays of light emanating from the cross, representing divine illumination, guidance, and the presence of God in our lives. Below the handshake, an olive branch is depicted, a timeless symbol of peace, victory, and hope from a life rooted in faith.

The surrounding images further elaborate on the diverse roles that men play within their families, communities, and workplaces, all grounded in a strong foundation of faith:

- **Barber Shop:** A traditional setting where men gather, not just for grooming but for conversation, wisdom, and community.
- **Mentor and Mentee:** Reflecting the importance of guidance, support, and the passing on wisdom from one generation to the next.
- **Pastor and Boy:** Symbolizing spiritual leadership, the pastor guides a young boy in faith and life, representing mentorship and nurturing in the spiritual journey.
- **Boys in the Hood:** Highlights the challenges and camaraderie among young men growing up in urban environments and the need for positive influences.
- **Students Studying:** Depicting the value of education, discipline, and the pursuit of knowledge as part of building a robust and informed character.
- **Grandfather and Grandson:** Emphasizing the deep bond and legacy shared between generations and the vital role of family in imparting values.
- **Fraternity Brothers:** symbolize brotherhood, unity, and a shared commitment to ideals that foster growth and mutual support.
- **Father and Son:** A representation of the crucial role of fathers in nurturing, teaching, and guiding their sons with love and discipline.
- **Soldiers:** Honoring the duty, sacrifice, and protection that come with service, embodying the principles of courage and steadfastness.

- **Fisherman:** An allusion to the biblical calling to be "fishers of men," symbolizing outreach, patience, and faith in action.
- **Office Coworkers:** Reflecting professionalism, collaboration, and the importance of integrity and respect in the workplace.
- **Bikers:** A portrayal of the bonds formed through shared experiences and journeys and the freedom of authentic living one's faith.
- **EMS, Firemen, Policemen:** Recognizing the commitment and bravery of those who serve and protect the community, often at significant personal risk.
- **Church Small Group Study:** Illustrating the power of fellowship, Bible study, and collective worship in strengthening faith and community bonds.
- **Coworkers:** Demonstrating the importance of teamwork, accountability, and mutual support in achieving common goals.
- **Athletes:** represent the discipline, perseverance, and teamwork required in sports, qualities that parallel the journey of faith

Combined with these images, the rays of light and olive branch create a visual narrative that speaks to the breadth of experiences and roles that Christian men navigate. These symbols remind us that faith, peace, and integrity principles should be lived out in every interaction and relationship, extending to all areas of life. This cover invites you to reflect on your journey, to grow intentionally, and to lead others by example, fostering a legacy of faith that will endure for generations.

INTRODUCTION
HOW TO USE THIS BOOK

"A godly man is one who submits to the authority of the Lord, embraces His Word as the foundation of life, and seeks to reflect Christ in every aspect of his daily walk."
– Charles Stanley.

Numbers 30:2 *"If a man vows a vow to the Lord, or swears an oath to bind himself by a pledge, he shall not break his word. He shall do according to all that proceeds out of his mouth."*

Who is This Book For?

If you can answer "**YES**" to any of these questions, this book is for you:

- Are you a male?
- Do you want to strengthen your relationship with God?
- Do you want to be a Godly man?
- Do you want to be a Godly husband/boyfriend?
- Do you want to be a Godly father?
- Do you want to be a Godly son, brother, uncle, cousin, co-worker, mentor, etc.?
- Do you want to disciple others?
- Do you want to reconnect with God?
- Do you want to be saved?

You can use this book in many ways: with a friend, in small groups, in men's ministries, during lunch breaks or coffee breaks, in barbershop talk, in prison ministry, in mentoring relationships, and in numerous other settings. While the book can be practical as a self-study, having an accountability partner or participating in a small group study is highly recommended. Engaging with others in this journey fosters deeper insights, mutual encouragement, and a richer experience as you hold each other accountable for living out the principles of Christian manhood. Central to these principles is the foundation of faith as seen in the lives of Joseph, Job, and Daniel and in the life of Jesus Christ, who provides the ultimate example of obedience, faithfulness, and love.

The lessons from Joseph, Job, and Daniel illustrate profound trust in God's plan, faith through suffering, and obedience in the face of trials—each pointing to the larger narrative of Jesus Christ's perfect life and sacrifice for mankind. These stories of faith build upon Christ's example and remind us that, as Christian men, we are called to live steadfastly on God's purpose for our lives.

However, if you study alone, this book will still guide you effectively, providing the tools and reflections needed to internalize and apply these commitments in your daily life. The examples from Joseph, Job, Daniel, and Jesus Christ will strengthen your journey, reminding you that God's presence and purpose are unwavering no matter the challenges.

The Foundation of Faith: Lessons from Joseph, Job, and Daniel

Regardless of where you find yourself in your spiritual journey—whether you are a new believer taking your first steps in faith or someone who has developed a steadfast trust in God, like that of a contemporary man of faith, such as a pastor who tirelessly serves his community or a mentor who embodies grace and resilience—this book holds valuable insights for you. Each stage of faith, from the innocence of a child in Christ to the profound wisdom of a seasoned believer, offers unique perspectives and experiences that can enrich your life through study and reflection.

Faith is the bedrock of a Christian man's life, a compass guiding him through the brightest days and the darkest nights. The Bible offers numerous examples of men who exhibited unwavering faith in the face of overwhelming trials. Among these, the stories of Joseph, Job, and Daniel stand out as profound testimonies of the power and necessity of faith. Their lives point us to the ultimate example of faith and obedience—Jesus Christ—whose life and sacrifice perfectly fulfill God's plan for redemption.

An Invitation to the Skeptical Brothers

To the brothers who may feel disconnected from God or harbor reservations about the church, I want you to know that I understand. Perhaps you've faced disappointment, seen hypocrisy, or felt judged by those who claim to walk in faith. If so, you're not alone. Many have wrestled with these same feelings and have felt lost, disillusioned, or misunderstood.

I encourage you to take this journey with us and explore the insights in this study. You don't need to have everything figured out, and you don't need to accept everything at face value. This journey offers an opportunity to approach faith with an open mind and heart, discovering the stories of men like Joseph, Job, and Daniel who faced real struggles yet found strength in something beyond themselves. My hope is that, as you complete this study, you'll find something meaningful and authentic—perhaps even a different perspective on faith and its place in your life.

Take this journey one step at a time, with honesty and curiosity. Know that you're welcome here, just as you are, with your questions and doubts.

The Struggles of Today's Man

In today's world, men face an array of complex challenges that test their strength, character, and resolve. Substance abuse is one of the most pervasive issues affecting men of all ages. Whether it's drugs, alcohol, or other addictive behaviors, these substances often provide a false escape from life's pressures but ultimately lead to broken relationships, deteriorated health, and, at times, despair. The journey to overcoming addiction is daunting, often marked by relapse and resilience. For men striving to honor God, substance abuse becomes a spiritual battle as much as it is a physical and mental one.

Relationships, too, pose significant challenges. Balancing the demands of family, work, and personal growth can create stress and strain. Relationships—whether with a spouse, children, friends, or colleagues—require commitment, sacrifice, and the willingness to listen and understand. Many men find themselves struggling to maintain meaningful connections or facing the pain of broken relationships. In a society where vulnerability is often discouraged in men, facing relational challenges openly can feel like an uphill battle.

Additionally, men today grapple with pressures around financial stability, career success, and mental health. The weight of providing, leading, and succeeding can be overwhelming, leading many men to internalize stress, anxiety, and even depression. The expectation to be "strong" often translates into silent suffering, as they feel unable to seek support or admit they need help.

This book acknowledges these challenges and offers a pathway toward healing, transformation, and growth. The Christian Manhood Pledge encourages men to face these obstacles with faith, integrity, and the support of a brotherhood committed to walking this journey together. You are not alone in your struggles. In the pages ahead, you will find practical steps and spiritual guidance to equip you to confront these trials and rise above them, empowering you to live a life that honors God and strengthens those around you.

Joseph: Faith in God's Plan

Joseph's journey from being a favored son to being sold as an enslaved person and eventually being appointed by Pharaoh as second in command over all of Egypt illustrates faith in God's sovereign plan. Joseph's faith in God's plan teaches us patience and trust, reminding us that God's timing is perfect and His plans are always for our good, even when the path is difficult.

Job: Faith in Suffering

Job's life is a powerful testament to the strength of faith amid suffering. Stripped of his wealth, health, and family, Job faced unimaginable trials that would have broken most men. Yet, despite his immense pain and the seeming silence of God, Job did not lose his faith. He questioned and wrestled with doubt but never turned his back on God. Job's faith teaches us that true faith involves holding on to God steadfastly, even when doubt, suffering, and loss are present.

Daniel: Faith in Obedience

Daniel's life is a shining example of faith rooted in obedience to God. Living in a foreign land under the rule of pagan kings, Daniel remained faithful to God's commandments. Even

Introduction How to Use This Book

when faced with death in the lion's den, Daniel chose to obey God rather than succumb to the pressures of the world around him. His story reminds us that faith requires not just belief but action—obedience to God's will, even when it is unpopular or dangerous.

Whether you're a father guiding your son, a grandfather sharing wisdom with your grandson, an uncle supporting your nephew, a Godfather mentoring your Godson, or a brother engaging with fellow church members, *The Christian Manhood Pledge* offers valuable insights for every relationship. Its teachings extend beyond family ties to mentorship in church groups, community gatherings, sports teams, or workplaces. Strengthening bonds with cousins, neighbors, or co-workers, guiding youth leaders, and actively participating in community efforts enhance the impact of the principles discussed in this book, encouraging growth and unity in every sphere of life.

In every interaction and relationship, the lessons of faith from Joseph, Job, and Daniel offer a solid foundation to build your faith. As you apply these timeless principles, may you find strength, wisdom, and encouragement to navigate your journey with steadfast faith, knowing that no matter the challenges, God's presence and purpose are unwavering. This book invites you to reflect deeply, grow intentionally, and lead others by example, fostering a legacy of faith that will endure from generation to generation.

To obtain further information about Joseph, Job, and Daniel, you can find their stories in the following books of the Bible:

- **Joseph**: Genesis (chapters 37-50)
- **Job**: The Book of Job
- **Daniel**: The Book of Daniel

For more profound inspiration and a greater understanding of faith, I encourage you to explore **Hebrews 11** in the Bible, often called the **'Hall of Faith.'** In this powerful chapter, you'll discover remarkable examples of unwavering faith lived out through the lives of biblical figures, offering further guidance and encouragement for your faith journey.

Additionally, *The Christian Manhood Pledge* is a powerful tool for ministering to non-believers or those who identify as spiritual but not religious. Its universal themes of love, integrity, and community engagement resonate with individuals seeking meaning and connection, regardless of their beliefs. By exploring this book's principles, you can initiate meaningful conversations that spark curiosity and openness. These principles foster genuine and respectful discussions about faith, allowing for deeper connections. These relationships will enhance your experience and contribute to growth and unity in your spiritual journey.

To further enhance your journey, consider partnering with an accountability partner. Studying alongside someone you trust can provide motivation and encouragement as you apply the principles learned. This relationship will help you stay committed to your growth while allowing open discussions about your experiences and insights.

The Value of Accountability

Accountability partners play an essential and invaluable role.

1. **Encouragement and Motivation:** Having an accountability partner provides encouragement and motivation. When you face challenges or feel discouraged, your partner can uplift and motivate you to stay committed to your pledges.

2. **Honest Feedback:** An accountability partner offers honest feedback and constructive criticism, helping you identify areas for improvement and providing insights you might have yet to consider.

3. **Shared Wisdom:** By studying and discussing the pledges together, you can share wisdom and experiences, learn from each other's journeys, and gain new perspectives.

4. **Spiritual Support:** An accountability partner can pray with and for you, providing spiritual support and helping you to seek God's guidance and strength in your endeavors.

5. **Consistency:** Regular meetings or check-ins with an accountability partner help maintain consistency in your commitment, ensuring that you stay on track and progress.

6. **Sense of Community:** Studying with others fosters a sense of community and belonging, creating a supportive environment where you can grow together and build lasting relationships.

Introduction How to Use This Book

How to Get the Most Out of This Book

To get the most out of this book, follow these steps:

1. **Read Each Chapter Thoroughly:** Take your time to understand the context and meaning behind each pledge. Reflect on how these principles apply to your own life.

2. **Engage with the Exercises:** Participate actively in the exercises and reflections provided in each chapter. These exercises help you think deeply and practically about implementing each pledge. For additional support, some exercises will reference the Appendices, where you can find further resources and guidance to supplement your journey.

3. **Journal Your Journey:** Use a notebook or journal to record your thoughts, progress, and challenges. Writing down your experiences will help reinforce your commitment and allow you to track your growth over time.

4. **Seek Accountability:** Share your journey with a trusted friend, mentor, or a small group. Having someone to discuss your progress with can provide encouragement and accountability.

5. **Pray for Guidance:** Consistently seek God's guidance and strength through prayer. Remember that this journey is about personal growth, deepening your relationship with God, and aligning your life with His will.

Using this book as your guide will equip you to uphold *The Christian Manhood Pledge* with conviction and integrity. Together, we can strive to live out these pledges and positively impact our families, communities, and the world.

Commemorate Your Study Journey

As you conclude your journey through *The Christian Manhood Pledge* in the Conclusion, I invite you to formalize your commitment by creating a personalized certificate. In this final chapter, you will find detailed instructions and a QR code that, when scanned, will take you to *The Manhood Institute website*. You and your accountability partner(s) can enter your names and signatures to commemorate *The Christian Manhood Pledge* there.

Once you've completed the form, you can generate an 8 1/2 x 11 PDF certificate to print or download. This certificate serves as a lasting symbol of your commitment. You can display it as a testament to your dedication to living out the principles outlined in

7

The Christian Manhood Pledge. Whether framed or kept in a visible place, it will be a daily reminder of your promises and the strength you draw from God.

The Christian Manhood Pledge

In the presence of Almighty God, I, [Your Name], solemnly make the following pledges, drawing upon the Scripture for guidance and strength:

Love and Devotion: "In the sight of the Lord, I make this pledge: to love the Lord my God with all my heart, soul, mind, and strength, and to love my neighbor as myself, as it is written in **Mark 12:30-31**. I commit to spiritual, moral, mental, social, political, and economic growth, guided by **Proverbs 16:3**. This endeavor is for the betterment of my family and community, in accordance with **1 Corinthians 10:24**."

Diligence and Prosperity: "I pledge to follow the path of diligence and enterprise, as encouraged in **Proverbs 14:23**. I will engage in lawful commerce and contribute to the prosperity of my people, following the example set forth in **Deuteronomy 8:18**."

Protection and Love: "With a steadfast heart, I vow never to harm another, recalling the teachings of **Exodus 20:13**. I will cherish and protect my family, as stated in **Ephesians 5:25** and admonished in **Ephesians 6:4** to bring up my children in the discipline and instruction of the Lord."

Defender of Childhood: "I solemnly declare to defend the innocence of childhood," echoing **Matthew 18:6**. I will nurture and protect the purity of our youth, as affirmed by **Psalm 127:3**.

Honoring and Uplifting Women: "I renounce derogatory language against women, following the wisdom of **Colossians 3:8**. I pledge to honor and uplift the women of my community, as commanded in **1 Peter 3:7**."

Health and Purity: "I vow to safeguard my body, the temple of the Holy Spirit, as instructed in **1 Corinthians 6:19-20 and 10:31**, committing to glorify God in all that I do."

Community Support and Unity: "I commit to supporting and uplifting my community with unwavering dedication, inspired by **Romans 15:2** and **Philippians 2:4**, striving to promote positivity and unity."

Divine Strength and Guidance: "In making these pledges, I seek the strength and guidance of Almighty God, acknowledging that my own power can accomplish none of this. As stated in **Philippians 4:13**, '*I can do all things through Him who strengthens me.*' This declaration is a statement of intent and a prayer for endurance, wisdom, and courage to live out these commitments. So help me God."

Pre-Evaluation: Confidence in Fulfilling the Pledges

Instructions:

Before starting the book, assess where you currently stand for each pledge. Use the scale below to select the word that best reflects your confidence in fulfilling each pledge. For each pledge, **circle the scale** that best reflects your confidence in fulfilling that pledge.

Scale		
1	Struggling	I have little to no knowledge or experience; it's a challenge for me.
2	Building	I have some knowledge but still need help to improve.
3	Developing	I have a good foundation and am growing; there's still more to learn.
4	Strong	I am confident and knowledgeable in fulfilling this pledge.

Pledges	Confidence Level			
Love and Devotion	1	2	3	4
Diligence and Prosperity	1	2	3	4
Protection and Love	1	2	3	4
Defender of Childhood	1	2	3	4
Honoring and Uplifting Women	1	2	3	4
Health and Purity	1	2	3	4
Community Support and Unity	1	2	3	4
Divine Strength and Guidance	1	2	3	4

Accountability Partner Commitment

As part of this study, please identify your accountability partner below. Both you and your partner should sign and date this section as a commitment to supporting each other throughout the journey.

Accountability Partner's Name: _____

Your Name: _____

Date: _____

Signatures:

Accountability Partner's Signature: _____

Your Signature: _____

As we conclude this introduction, I want to leave you with this prayer:

Heavenly Father,

I come before You with gratitude for the reader who is about to embark on this journey of understanding and commitment through *The Christian Manhood Pledge*. Please pour out Your wisdom and insight upon him as he delves into the teachings and reflections within these pages.

Lord, grant him the discernment to grasp the deeper meanings and the courage to embrace the lessons that will challenge and transform him. May his heart be open to Your guidance, and may he find clarity in the truths You reveal through this study.

I pray that You keep him focused and engaged, not just in reading but in genuinely absorbing and reflecting on the principles of Christian manhood. Let this journey be more than an intellectual exercise. Let it be a transformative experience that shapes his character and strengthens his faith.

Encourage him, Father, as he navigates through each chapter. May he find inspiration in every word, motivation in every challenge, and strength in every truth. Guide him to apply what he learns, not only to his thoughts but to his actions, so that he may live out these principles with integrity and conviction.

As he walks this path, I ask that You bless his relationship with his accountability partner. May they support and uplift each other, growing together in faith and commitment. Let their partnership be a source of mutual encouragement, accountability, and spiritual growth, drawing them closer to You.

Lord, may this study be a source of joy and fulfillment, deepening his relationship with You and improving every aspect of his life. Let it ignite a passion for Your Word and a commitment to living out the values of Christian manhood.

Thank You for the opportunity to grow in wisdom and grace through the **"The Christian Manhood Pledge."** I ask for Your blessing, protection, and guidance over him and his accountability partner as they begin this journey together.

In Jesus' name, Amen.

CHAPTER 1

LOVE AND DEVOTION

Love encapsulates the fullness of God, Jesus, the Holy Spirit, the Bible, the Church, and the essence of Christianity itself.
- Michael Mauney

"In the sight of the Lord, I make this pledge: to love the Lord my God with all my heart, soul, mind, and strength, and to love my neighbor as myself, as it is written in Mark 12:30-31. I commit to spiritual, moral, mental, social, political, and economic growth, guided by Proverbs 16:3. This endeavor is for the betterment of my family and community, in accordance with 1 Corinthians 10:24."

Mark 12:30-31: *"And you shall love the Lord your God with all your heart and with all your soul and with all your mind and with all your strength. The second is this: You shall love your neighbor as yourself. There is no other commandment greater than these."*

Proverbs 16:3: *"Commit your work to the Lord, and your plans will be established."*

1 Corinthians 10:24: *"Let no one seek his own good, but the good of his neighbor."*

Loving God with All Your Heart, Soul, Mind, and Strength

In **Mark 12:30-31**, Jesus gives us the greatest commandments: to *"love the Lord your God with all your heart, soul, mind, and strength,"* and to *"love your neighbor as yourself."* This holistic love for God involves devoting every part of our being—our emotions, will, intellect, and physical actions—to glorifying Him. It's a profound commitment that shapes how we engage with the world and those around us.

1. **Heart**: Loving God with all your heart is more than just feelings; it's about placing Him above everything else. It means aligning your desires with His will, expressing gratitude, and continually seeking to please Him in all areas of life.

2. **Soul**: The soul represents your innermost being—your identity and purpose. To love God with all your soul requires fully surrendering your will, aligning your mission in life with His purposes, and reflecting His love, grace, and holiness through your character.

3. **Mind**: Loving God with all your mind involves actively seeking to know Him through His Word, reflecting on His truth, and applying wisdom in your daily decisions. It's about letting God's teachings shape your understanding and your thoughts about the world.

4. **Strength**: Loving God with all your strength means serving Him with your actions, energy, and resources. It's about putting faith into motion through service, obedience, and perseverance in the work God has given you.

When we commit our heart, soul, mind, and strength to God, love for others naturally flows from that devotion. Loving our neighbors becomes an extension of our love for God, fulfilling both commandments.

The Call to Love Your Neighbor

In the Gospel of Mark, Jesus delivers a command that resonates through the ages: *"You shall love your neighbor as yourself"* **Mark 12:31.** This directive is simple and profound, encapsulating the essence of Christian living. It serves as the cornerstone of *The Christian Manhood Pledge*. As men of faith, we embrace the call to understand and demonstrate love in our actions, attitudes, and interactions with others.

In the sight of the Lord, I make this pledge: to love the Lord my God with all my heart, soul, mind, and strength, and to love my neighbor as myself. I commit to spiritual, moral, mental, social, political, and economic growth for the betterment of my family and community.

The Nature of Love

Love is more than a fleeting emotion; it is an intentional, active choice. Loving our neighbor requires empathy, kindness, and a commitment to others' well-being. It means recognizing those around us not as obstacles or strangers but as fellow beings created in God's image, deserving respect and compassion.

To truly love our neighbors, we must first understand what this love looks like. It is a love that sacrifices, putting the needs of others above our own. In 1 John 3:18, we are reminded, 'Little children, let us not love in word or talk but in deed and in truth.' This verse calls us to action—inviting us to move beyond words and engage the world around us in meaningful, impactful ways.

The Challenge of Loving Others

Loving our neighbors is not always easy. It requires us to confront our biases, prejudices, and selfish tendencies. We live in a society that often promotes division, competition, and self-interest, making the practice of love feel like an uphill battle. Yet, in these moments of difficulty, our commitment to love is tested and strengthened.

As Christian men, we embrace the call to be leaders—not only in our families and workplaces but also in our communities. Authentic leadership involves understanding others' struggles and stepping outside our comfort zones to help those in need. Whether offering a listening ear, volunteering time, or standing up for justice, every act of love helps build a more compassionate and connected society.

Practical Steps to Love Your Neighbor

1. **Listen Actively**: Take time to listen to those around you genuinely. Active listening fosters trust and demonstrates that you value the thoughts and feelings of others. Ask open-ended questions and engage in meaningful conversations.

2. **Serve Others**: Look for opportunities to serve your community. Whether volunteering at a shelter, helping a neighbor with a task, or participating in local events, serving is a tangible way to show love.

3. **Practice Forgiveness**: No one is perfect, and we will inevitably hurt one another. Forgiving is a powerful act of love that promotes healing and reconciliation in relationships.

4. **Support Local Businesses**: Prioritizing local commerce strengthens the economy and builds community ties. Relationships with local shop owners and customers foster a sense of mutual support.

5. **Advocate for Justice**: Stand up for those who are marginalized or oppressed. Use your voice to advocate for equality and fairness and support initiatives that promote justice.

6. **Pray for Others**: Commit to praying for your neighbors, friends, and even those you find challenging to love. Prayer invites God into the situation and helps cultivate a heart of compassion.

Reflecting Christ's Love

At the heart of loving our neighbors is the example of Christ. Throughout His ministry, Jesus exemplified selfless love—healing the sick, feeding the hungry, and reaching out to the marginalized. As we follow His example, we should reflect on His love daily.

In **John 13:34-35**, Jesus offers a new commandment: *"A new commandment I give to you, that you love one another: just as I have loved you, you also are to love one another. By this, all people will know that you are my disciples if you have love for one another."* Our love for others is a powerful testimony of our faith and devotion to Christ.

The Greatest Commandments: Loving God, Others, and Yourself

In **Mark 12:30-31**, Jesus commands us: *"And you shall love the Lord your God with all your heart and with all your soul and with all your mind and with all your strength."* The second is this: *"You shall love your neighbor as yourself."* There is no other commandment greater than these.' These words are often understood to focus on loving God and loving others. However, Jesus also says, 'as you love yourself,' pointing to the importance of a healthy, God-honoring love of self. Many sermons and lessons emphasize loving God and others. Still, Jesus indicates that a positive love for oneself is essential. When rightly understood, this self-love provides the foundation for loving others well.

Loving Yourself in a God-Honoring Way

In today's world, self-love is often confused with selfishness or self-centeredness, where people put their needs above everyone else's. However, this is not the kind of self-love that Jesus teaches. The Bible does not encourage a love that leads to pride, entitlement, or placing oneself before others. Instead, it teaches a self-love rooted in recognizing your worth as a child of God and honoring yourself as a unique part of His creation.

Loving yourself in a positive, God-honoring way means recognizing that you are *"fearfully and wonderfully made"* **Psalm 139:14**. It means caring for your body, mind, and spirit because neglecting these is to dishonor the life God has given you. It's about having a humble appreciation for who you are in Christ, acknowledging your value in His eyes, and knowing that your purpose is to serve others.

This healthy self-love enables you to love others more fully. It can be hard to love others well if you don't see yourself as worthy or capable. But when you appreciate yourself in a humble, balanced way, you are better equipped to love others and reflect God's love in your actions.

The Importance of Self-Care in Diligence

Determining to serve God and others also requires caring for yourself, including your physical health, mental well-being, and spiritual life. Even Jesus modeled the importance of self-care, often withdrawing to rest and pray **Mark 1:35**. If we don't renew ourselves, we risk burnout and become less effective in our service to others.

Proper diligence involves finding balance—taking time to rest in God's presence, nurturing your relationship with Him, and maintaining overall well-being. As you devote yourself to loving God and others, remember you cannot give from an empty cup. By caring for yourself in a healthy, God-centered way, you strengthen your ability to love your neighbor as Jesus commanded.

Committing Your Work to the Lord

Proverbs 16:3 reminds us to *"Commit your work to the Lord, and your plans will be established."* This verse emphasizes the importance of aligning our actions and ambitions with God's will. When we devote our spiritual, personal, or professional endeavors to God, we can trust that He will guide our steps and bring about success according to His divine purpose. As men striving for Christian manhood, this commitment is vital. It's a call to make our work an offering to God, seeking His guidance in every area of our lives. By doing so, we invite God into the process, knowing that true success comes when our plans are rooted in Him.

Seeking the Good of Others

In **1 Corinthians 10:24**, the Bible teaches us, *"Let no one seek his own good, but the good of his neighbor."* This powerful message encourages us to live selflessly, placing the needs of others before our own. True Christian manhood means pursuing personal growth while uplifting those around us. It is a call to compassion and generosity, reflecting Christ's love in how we serve and support our neighbors. Whether through simple acts of kindness or more significant efforts to bring about justice and change, we fulfill our duty as Christian men by prioritizing the well-being of others over our self-interest.

Conclusion

The call to love our neighbor is an ideal and profound mandate that shapes our identity as Christian men. As we commit to living out **The Greatest Commandments: Loving God, Loving Others, and Loving Yourself**, we must continually seek God's guidance and strength. This balanced love enables us to reflect Christ's heart in our lives, impacting our families, communities, and world.

Always remember that true love is a feeling and a commitment to action. When we love God with all our heart, soul, mind, and strength, love our neighbors, and love ourselves in a healthy, God-honoring way, we equip ourselves to serve and uplift those around us. As we go forth into our communities, may we carry the heart of Christ— seeking to support, love, and encourage others. In doing so, we fulfill our pledge and become the men God has called us to be.

Love and Devotion

EXERCISES FOR REFLECTION AND ACTION

1. Personal Reflection on Loving God

Reflect on each aspect of loving God with all your heart, soul, mind, and strength. Consider how you can grow in these areas and deepen your relationship with Him.

Objective: Reflect on how you can actively love God with all your heart, soul, mind, and strength, and find practical ways to extend that love to your neighbor.

	Response
1. Heart:	How can you prioritize God in your affections and desires this week?
	What are specific ways you can express gratitude and trust in Him?
2. Soul:	Reflect on how your life's mission and purpose align with God's will.
	Are there areas of your life that need more surrender to His plan?
3. Mind:	What steps can you take to better engage with God's Word and let it shape your thoughts?
	How can you apply godly wisdom in your daily decisions?
4. Strength:	How can you use your energy, resources, and talents to serve God and others more effectively this week?

19

The Christian Manhood Pledge

2. Personal Inventory

Take time to reflect on your relationships with those around you. Write down three people in your life you feel you could love better. Consider specific actions you can take this week to show them love, whether through a kind word, a small gift, or simply spending quality time with them.

Objective: Reflect on your relationships and identify opportunities to express love more intentionally toward those around you.

Response
1. **Person One:**
2. **Person Two:**
3. **Person Three:**

Love and Devotion

3. Community Engagement Challenge

Identify a local organization or a cause that is meaningful to you. Commit to volunteering your time or contributing resources at least once a month for the next three months. After every encounter, give yourself some time to consider how your participation has influenced both the community and your development.

Objective: Reflect on your relationships and identify opportunities to express love more intentionally toward those around you.

Response	
1.	**Organization/Cause:**
2.	**Goal:**
3.	**Reflection:**

The Christian Manhood Pledge

4. Forgiveness Journal

Create a journal dedicated to the theme of forgiveness. Write about any past hurts you hold onto and people you must forgive. Commit to praying for these individuals and asking God to help you release bitterness. Consider reaching out to those you can reconcile with and taking steps toward healing.

Objective: Reflect on past hurts and commit to forgiveness, seeking healing and reconciliation through prayer and intentional actions.

Response	
1.	**Past hurts:**
2.	**Individuals to forgive:**
3.	**Actions for reconciliation:**

Love and Devotion

4.	Prayers for healing:

BY ACTIVELY ENGAGING IN THESE MEANINGFUL EXERCISES,
WE CAN DEEPEN OUR COMMITMENT TO LOVING GOD WITH
ALL OUR HEART, SOUL, MIND, AND STRENGTH WHILE BUILDING
MORE ROBUST, COMPASSIONATE RELATIONSHIPS WITH OUR
NEIGHBORS. THROUGH THESE ACTIONS, WE IMPACT OUR
FAMILIES, COMMUNITIES, AND THE WORLD, EMBODYING THE LOVE
AND LEADERSHIP THAT CHRIST HAS CALLED US TO LIVE OUT.

NOTES

CHAPTER 2

DILIGENCE AND PROSPERITY

"You are never too old to set another goal or to dream a new dream."
-C.S. Lewis

"I pledge to follow the path of diligence and enterprise, as encouraged in Proverbs 14:23. I will engage in lawful commerce and contribute to the prosperity of my people, following the example set forth in Deuteronomy 8:18

Proverbs 14:23: *"In all toil there is profit, but mere talk tends only to poverty."*

Deuteronomy 8:18: *"You shall remember the Lord your God, for it is he who gives you power to get wealth, that he may confirm his covenant that he swore to your fathers, as it is this day."*

This pledge underscores the importance of hard work and responsibility in pursuing growth and excellence.

"Commit your work to the Lord, and your plans will be established" **Proverbs 16:3.** This simple yet profound verse lays the foundation for a life dedicated to growth—spiritual, moral, mental, social, political, and economic. As Christian men, we embrace the call to pursue personal growth and to support the development of those around us. Our journey toward maturity and excellence begins with a conscious commitment to work diligently in all aspects of life, grounded in faith.

The Importance of Holistic Growth

Growth is not a one-dimensional process; it requires nurturing multiple facets of our lives. A well-rounded man strives to improve spiritually, morally, mentally, socially, politically, and economically. Each of these areas is interconnected, and neglecting one can hinder progress in the other.

1. **Spiritual Growth:** This foundation supports all other growth. A robust spiritual life nourishes our faith and informs our decisions. Engaging in regular prayer, studying Scripture, and participating in communal worship are vital practices that deepen our relationship with God. Spiritual growth equips us to face life's challenges with resilience and wisdom.

2. **Moral Growth:** Our moral compass guides our actions and decisions. As we seek moral growth, we must align our values with biblical principles by cultivating honesty, integrity, and humility. Reflecting on passages like **Proverbs 4:7**, which states, *"The beginning of wisdom is this: Get wisdom, and whatever you get, get insight,"* reminds us to pursue moral excellence actively.

3. **Mental Growth:** We can achieve personal development by actively engaging our minds through continuous learning, reading, and critical thinking. The pursuit of knowledge and understanding not only enriches our lives but also equips us to contribute effectively to our families and communities. *"Iron sharpens iron, and one man sharpens another"* **Proverbs 27:17** illustrates the importance of surrounding ourselves with others who encourage our growth.

4. **Social Growth:** Our relationships with others are essential for a fulfilling life. Building strong, healthy relationships involves developing communication skills, empathy, and emotional intelligence. **Acts 2:44-47** describes the early church's commitment to community, encouraging us to engage with those around us, share our lives, and foster a sense of Economic growth of belonging.

5. **Political Growth:** As responsible citizens, we must understand the political landscape and advocate for justice and righteousness. Engaging in political discourse, voting, and supporting policies that align with our values are crucial steps in this process. **Micah 6:8** challenges us to *"do justice, love kindness, and walk humbly with our God,"* reminding us of our responsibility to advocate for others.

6. **Economic Growth:** Pursuing economic stability and growth allows us to provide for our families and contribute to our communities. Economic development involves wise stewardship of resources, ethical business practices, and the willingness to support local economies. **Deuteronomy 8:18** reminds us to recognize that God gives us the power to obtain wealth, encouraging us to approach our work with gratitude and integrity.

Setting Goals and Taking Action

We must set clear, actionable goals to commit to growth in these areas. Begin by assessing where you are in each aspect of your life and identifying areas for improvement. Consider these steps:

1. **Create a Personal Development Plan:** Outline specific goals for spiritual, moral, mental, social, political, and economic growth. Break these goals down into manageable steps and set timelines for achieving them.

2. **Engage in Accountability:** Find a mentor or a group of like-minded individuals who can encourage and hold you accountable in your growth journey. Sharing your goals with others can foster a sense of commitment and support.

3. **Reflect Regularly:** Set aside time for self-reflection to evaluate your progress. Are you growing as you intended? Are there areas where you need to adjust your focus? Reflection allows you to celebrate successes and learn from setbacks.

4. **Invest in Resources:** Seek out books, courses, and workshops to help your development. Whether it's a Bible study, a leadership seminar, or a personal finance workshop, the right resources can accelerate your growth.

5. **Stay Open to Change:** Growth often requires stepping outside your comfort zone. Be willing to embrace new experiences and perspectives, recognizing that change can lead to personal and spiritual transformation.

The Role of Faith in Growth

At the heart of our commitment to growth is our relationship with God. We must rely on His guidance and strength as we seek to grow. **Philippians 4:13** reassures us: *"I can do all things through him who strengthens me."* Our growth journey is not solely about our efforts but about surrendering to God's will and allowing Him to work in us.

When we face challenges, we can turn to Scripture for encouragement. **James 1:5** encourages us to ask God for wisdom, assuring us that He will provide. This wisdom guides our decisions and illuminates our path, helping us navigate the complexities of life with grace.

The Value of Hard Work and Responsibility

As we journey toward growth and excellence, hard work and responsibility are essential. The Bible consistently affirms the rewards of diligent labor, reminding us that effort and perseverance are vital components of success. **Proverbs 14:23** says, *"In all toil there is profit, but mere talk leads only to poverty."* This passage emphasizes that words alone do not bring prosperity; it is through committed action that we see tangible results.

Taking responsibility for our actions and decisions is also central to growth. Whether it is our personal, spiritual, or professional life, we are accountable to God, ourselves, and those we influence. As men of faith, we embrace the call to work diligently, not just for our gain but for the benefit of our families, communities, and society at large. When we align our work with God's purpose, our labor becomes an act of worship and a reflection of our commitment to excellence.

Conclusion

Commitment to growth is a lifelong journey that requires intentionality, perseverance, and hard work. Christian men embrace the call to continually seek improvement in every area of their lives and the responsibility that comes with it. By dedicating ourselves to holistic growth and putting in the diligent effort required, we honor our pledge and exemplify the values of our faith.

Let us remember that growth is not a destination but a process. Fueled by commitment and hard work, each step brings us closer to the men God has designed us to be. By committing our work to the Lord, embracing responsibility, and striving for excellence, we can become beacons of hope and inspiration to those around us, fulfilling our purpose in Christ.

EXERCISES FOR REFLECTION AND ACTION

1. Personal Growth Inventory

Reflect on each area of growth discussed in this chapter (spiritual, moral, mental, social, political, and economic). Rate yourself on a scale of 1-10 in each area and write down specific goals for improvement in at least two of these aspects.

Objective: Assess your personal development across key areas and set specific goals for improvement to foster balanced growth.

Response
For each area of growth listed below, please circle the number that best reflects your current level of development on a scale of 1 to 10, with 1 being the lowest and 10 being the highest.

Spiritual Growth	1 2 3 4 5 6 7 8 9 10
Moral Growth	1 2 3 4 5 6 7 8 9 10
Mental Growth	1 2 3 4 5 6 7 8 9 10

Goals for Improvement

1. Spiritual Growth:

2. Moral Growth:

3.	Mental Growth:

4.	Social Growth:

5.	Political Growth:

6.	Economic Growth:

2. Community Engagement Challenge

Identify a local issue or need you can contribute to through service or advocacy. Set a goal to act in this area at least once a month for the next three months. Reflect on how this experience enhances your understanding of social and political growth.

Diligence and Prosperity

Objective: Actively contribute to a local issue or need through service or advocacy. Reflect on how this involvement deepens your understanding of social and political growth.

Response
1. **Issue/Need:**
2. **Action Plan:**
3. **Reflection:**

The Christian Manhood Pledge

3. Economic Stewardship Plan

Consider your current financial practices and how they align with your commitment to economic growth and ethical stewardship. Write down three specific actions you can take to improve your financial management or support local businesses.

Objective: Reflect on your financial practices and develop specific actions to enhance financial management and support economic growth through ethical stewardship.

Response	
1.	**Action:**
2.	**Action:**
3.	**Action:**

Diligence and Prosperity

4. Accountability Partnership

Take time to share your growth goals with your accountability partner. Discuss your aspirations in one or more of the areas of growth covered in this chapter. Schedule regular check-ins to encourage each other and hold one another accountable.

Objective: Establish a supportive relationship with a mentor or peer to share growth goals, provide mutual encouragement, and maintain accountability through regular check-ins.

Response	
1.	**Accountability Partner Name:**
2.	**Growth Areas Discussed:**
3.	**Next Check-in Date:**

33

The Christian Manhood Pledge

5. Spiritual Growth Reflection

Set aside time for prayer and reflection. Write down one specific area where God calls you to grow spiritually. Commit to one action you can take this week to deepen your faith.

Objective: Engage in prayer and reflection to identify an area for spiritual growth and commit to actionable steps to deepen your faith.

Response	
1.	**Area of Spiritual Growth:**
2.	**Action for Growth:**

Diligence and Prosperity

BY ACTIVELY ENGAGING IN THESE MEANINGFUL EXERCISES, WE CAN STRENGTHEN OUR COMMITMENT TO PERSONAL GROWTH, HARD WORK, AND RESPONSIBILITY IN ALL AREAS OF LIFE. AS WE STRIVE FOR EXCELLENCE, WE GROW AS INDIVIDUALS AND CONTRIBUTE TO THE WELL-BEING OF OUR FAMILIES AND COMMUNITIES, REFLECTING THE VALUES OF *THE CHRISTIAN MANHOOD PLEDGE*.

NOTES

CHAPTER 3

PROTECTION AND LOVE

> *"Nonviolence is a powerful and just weapon which cuts without wounding and ennobles the man who wields it."*
> **- Martin Luther King Jr.**

"With a steadfast heart, I vow never to harm another, recalling the teachings of Exodus 20:13. I will cherish and protect my family, as stated in Ephesians 5:25 and admonished in Ephesians 6:4 to bring up my children in the discipline and instruction of the Lord.

Exodus 20:13 *"You shall not murder."*

Ephesians 5:25 *"Husbands, love your wives, as Christ loved the church and gave himself up for her."*

Ephesians 6:4 *"Fathers, do not provoke your children to anger, but bring them up in the discipline and instruction of the Lord."*

In our journey of Christian manhood, the principles of non-violence and family protection are pillars of our faith and commitment. Christian men embrace the call to continually seek improvement in every area of their lives and the responsibility that comes with it. As men of God, we are called to embody Christ's teachings in our actions, fostering a loving environment within our homes and communities. The Scriptures provide clear guidance on how we can fulfill our roles as protectors, nurturing our families and spirits through non-violent means.

The Call to Non-Violence

Exodus 20:13 reminds us of the sanctity of life with the commandment, *"You shall not murder."* This instruction goes beyond the literal act of taking a life; it implores us to cultivate a spirit of peace and compassion. Non-violence is not merely the absence of physical harm; it encompasses our words, thoughts, and attitudes toward others. As Christian men, we strive to create an atmosphere where respect and love prevail, recognizing that every individual is made in the image of God.

Embracing Christ-Like Love

Ephesians 5:25 calls on husbands to love their wives as Christ loved the church. This love is sacrificial and nurturing, aimed at the growth and well-being of our families. Christ's love is gentle yet firm, guiding us to act with wisdom and grace. Cultivating this type of love in our marriages creates a foundation of trust and safety, allowing our families to flourish.

Moreover, **Ephesians 6:4** instructs fathers to raise their children in a manner that does not provoke them to anger but instead fosters a loving, disciplined environment rooted in the teachings of the Lord. Christ-like love requires patience, understanding, and the ability to communicate effectively. God calls us to guide our children, offering them a sense of security that comes from knowing they are loved and valued.

The Protective Heart

To protect our families, we must first protect our hearts from anger, frustration, and resentment. Our ability to respond with love and compassion begins with a solid spiritual foundation. As we align our hearts with God's teachings, we are better equipped to create a haven for our loved ones.

Building a Culture of Non-Violence

Creating a culture of non-violence within our families begins with our attitudes and behaviors. We must model the behavior we wish to see in our children, demonstrating conflict resolution through dialogue rather than aggression. Encouraging open communication fosters an environment where everyone feels heard and valued, ultimately reducing the likelihood of conflict.

Strengthening Our Communities Through Non-Violence

As men of faith, our influence extends beyond the walls of our homes and into our communities. A commitment to non-violence equips us to be peacemakers, as Jesus urged in **Matthew 5:9**: *"Blessed are the peacemakers, for they shall be called sons of God."* Christian men can lead by example in a world fraught with conflict, demonstrating how to resolve conflicts peacefully and respectfully. Our families, neighbors, and even colleagues observe our behavior. By cultivating peace in every sphere of our lives, we strengthen our families and the communities we live in. Our actions become a testament to God's love, opening doors for others to see the power of Christian manhood rooted in love and peace.

Guarding Our Tongues as a Form of Non-Violence

Non-violence encompasses not only our physical actions but also the words we speak. **James 1:19** urges us to *"be quick to listen, slow to speak, and slow to anger."* Words have the power to build or destroy relationships. As men called to lead, we must be mindful of how we communicate, especially during times of tension. Gentle words, seasoned with grace, reflect the heart of Christ and can diffuse potentially volatile situations. Learning to speak life into our families – affirming, encouraging, and offering words of wisdom – is critical to creating an atmosphere of trust and love. Let us guard our tongues and speak in ways that edify rather than harm, fostering peace in our homes.

Embracing Forgiveness as a Tool for Peace

Forgiveness is at the heart of non-violence and is crucial in maintaining healthy family dynamics. In **Colossians 3:13**, Paul reminds us to *"bear with each other and* *forgive one another."* There will be moments when misunderstandings arise or we feel wronged by our loved ones. In those moments, we choose either to respond in anger or to extend forgiveness, just as Christ forgives us. Choosing forgiveness over retaliation requires humility and strength. By fostering a spirit of forgiveness in our homes, we model the love of Christ, and we teach our families how to navigate conflicts with grace and compassion.

The Legacy of Non-Violence

Ultimately, our commitment to non-violence leaves a lasting legacy for future generations. Our children will carry forward the values we instill in them into their own families and communities. **Proverbs 22:6** states, '*Train up a child in the way he should go, and when he is old, he will not depart from it.*' By modeling non-violence, Christ-like love, and protection, we pass on a legacy of peace that can impact future generations. Our children will learn how to handle conflict, express love, and protect their families in ways that reflect God's heart. Passing on these values creates a legacy far more significant than any material inheritance, shaping the character and faith of those who follow in our footsteps.

Conclusion

This chapter explored the profound significance of non-violence and family protection in our Christian journey. By committing ourselves to the teachings of Scripture, we cultivate loving, nurturing relationships within our families and extend that peace into our communities. Embracing the call to be peacemakers in our homes and wherever we influence others means guarding our words, demonstrating forgiveness, and leading by example to foster environments where love and respect thrive. Our commitment to these principles is not just for the present but for future generations. By instilling values of non-violence, patience, and Christ-like love, we leave a legacy of peace for our children and their future families. Protecting our families means more than safeguarding them from external threats; it involves nurturing their hearts and guiding them through life's challenges with compassion and wisdom.

Take these principles to heart, remembering that our actions speak volumes. In embracing non-violence and demonstrating unwavering love for our families and communities, we reflect the character of Christ, ultimately leading those we love closer to Him and creating a lasting impact that resonates for generations.

Protection and Love

EXERCISES FOR REFLECTION AND ACTION

1. Personal Inventory of Non-Violence

Reflect on your interactions with family, friends, coworkers, and strangers. Consider times when your words or actions may have been hurtful, intentionally or unintentionally. Write down these instances, reflecting on how your behavior may have affected others. Then, consider how you could have approached each situation differently, embodying non-violence and empathy.

Objective: Reflect on past interactions to identify moments of hurtful behavior and explore how to approach similar situations with non-violence and compassion.

	Response
1.	**Instance One:**
	Description of Hurtful Action/Words:
	How You Could Have Handled It Differently:
2.	**Instance Two:**
	Description of Hurtful Action/Words:
	How It Could Have Been Handled Differently:

41

The Christian Manhood Pledge

3.	**Instance Three:**
	Description of Hurtful Action/Words:
	How It Could Have Been Handled Differently:

2. Creating a Family Mission Statement

Gather your family and create a mission statement emphasizing love, respect, and non-violence. Discuss what these values mean to you and how to practice them daily. Please write down your mission statement and display it prominently in your home.

Objective: Collaboratively develop a family mission statement emphasizing love, respect, and non-violence, and commit to practicing these values daily.

See Appendix A: Sample Family Mission Statement for guidance on creating your own.

Response	
Family Values Discussion	
1.	What does Love mean to each family member?
2.	What does Respect mean to each family member?

Protection and Love

3.	What does Non-Violence mean to each family member?

	Drafting the Mission Statement
1.	Our Family Mission Statement:

	Displaying the Mission Statement
2.	Where will you display it in your home?

3. Conflict Resolution Role-Play

With a family member, accountability partner, or friend, practice resolving a hypothetical conflict nonviolently by using 'I statements to express your feelings and needs without placing blame. Then, reflect on how this approach felt compared to past conflict resolutions.

Objective: Practice nonviolent conflict resolution using **"I"** statements to express feelings and needs and reflect on the effectiveness of this approach compared to previous methods.

For a practical application of conflict resolution techniques, please refer to **Appendix B: Conflict Resolution Role-Play** for an example exercise."

43

The Christian Manhood Pledge

Response
Conflict Resolution Role-Play

1. Scenario:

2. Role-Play:

3. Reflection:

BY ENGAGING IN THESE EXERCISES, WE CAN DEEPEN OUR COMMITMENT TO NON-VIOLENCE AND FAMILY PROTECTION, ENSURING THAT OUR HOMES REFLECT THE LOVE OF CHRIST IN EVERY INTERACTION.

NOTES

CHAPTER 4

DEFENDER OF CHILDHOOD

"Children are not only our greatest treasure but also our greatest responsibility. As fathers, we are called to protect their innocence and guide their hearts towards the love of Christ."
- Uknown Christian Father

"I solemnly declare to defend the innocence of childhood," echoing Matthew 18:6. I will nurture and protect the purity of our youth, as affirmed by Psalm 127:3.

Matthew 18:6: *"But whoever causes one of these little ones who believe in me to sin, it would be better for him to have a great millstone fastened around his neck and to be drowned in the depth of the sea."*

Psalm 127:3: *"Behold, children are a heritage from the Lord, the fruit of the womb a reward."*

As Christian men, we are profoundly responsible for nurturing and protecting our children's innocence. Our pledge to defend childhood innocence is a commitment and a calling grounded in Scripture. In **Matthew 18:6**, we are reminded of the seriousness of leading children astray. The weight of this warning compels us to create environments where our children can grow in faith and love, shielded from harm.

Embracing the Gift of Children

Psalm 127:3 beautifully illustrates that children are a heritage from the Lord—a gift to be cherished and protected. They are not merely our responsibility; they are our blessing. Each child carries immense potential and the capacity to impact the world. As stewards of this heritage, we must actively engage in their lives, ensuring their spiritual, emotional, and physical well-being.

The Role of a Protector

Protecting the innocence of our youth means more than shielding them from physical dangers; it also involves guarding their hearts and minds against negative influences. As fathers, mentors, and role models, we must create safe spaces where children can explore, ask questions, and learn about God's love. Our actions should reflect the love of Christ, showing them that they are valued and worthy of respect.

Nurturing Their Spiritual Growth

To uphold the sanctity of childhood, we must intentionally nurture our children's spiritual growth. Engaging them in discussions about faith, encouraging them to pray, and sharing Scripture can foster a solid spiritual foundation. Our involvement in their spiritual journey reinforces their understanding of God's love and purpose for their lives.

Guardians of Innocence in a Modern World

In today's world, the challenges to preserving childhood innocence have grown immensely. With the rapid rise of digital media and easy access to harmful content, the responsibility of protecting our children is more urgent than ever. As fathers and Christian men, we must remain vigilant, monitoring what our children consume and helping them discern right from wrong. **Proverbs 22:6** reminds us to *"train up a child in the way he should go,"* including teaching them to navigate the complexities of modern culture with wisdom and integrity. It is not enough to shield them from negative influences—we must also equip them with the tools to make godly choices when we are not there to guide them.

The Power of Example

Children learn from what we say and, more importantly, from what we do. Our actions must consistently reflect the values we wish to instill in them. If we seek to protect their innocence, we must model purity and righteousness in our own lives. In **1 Timothy 4:12**, Paul encourages believers to *"set an example in speech, in conduct, in love, in faith, and in purity."* Our children will imitate how we treat others, handle conflicts, and express love. As fathers and role models, we set a high standard of integrity and faithfulness for them to aspire to.

Cultivating Spiritual Discernment

While protecting our children's innocence, we are also responsible for developing their spiritual discernment. Innocence is not ignorance; it's a state of purity that comes with awareness of both good and evil. By teaching our children to understand right and wrong, we empower them to make godly decisions. **Philippians 4:8** guides us in this effort: *"Whatever is true, whatever is honorable, whatever is just, whatever is pure, whatever is lovely...think about these things."* Encouraging our children to focus on these virtues equips them with the spiritual discernment needed to remain innocent without being naive, enabling them to stand firm in their faith when faced with moral challenges.

Creating a Joyful Environment

Creating a joyful and engaging environment is essential as we commit to protecting our children. Laughter, play, and creativity are integral to childhood, allowing children to thrive and discover their gifts. By cultivating an atmosphere of joy and love, we help our children build resilience, self-esteem, and a lasting connection to their faith.

Building a Supportive Christian Community

Fathers are not alone in the task of protecting and nurturing the innocence of children. The church and the broader Christian community are vital in supporting families and creating environments where children can thrive. **Hebrews 10:24-25** reminds us to *"spur one another on toward love and good deeds, not giving up meeting together."* We must seek out and foster relationships with other Christian families who share our values, creating a support network for our children and us. Within this community, children can form healthy friendships and experience the joy of growing in faith alongside peers who encourage them to stay true to God's principles.

Conclusion

In this chapter, we have explored our sacred duty to defend childhood innocence. By nurturing and protecting our children, we honor God's gift and reflect His love in their lives. Our commitment to creating a safe, joyful, and spiritually enriching environment will empower the next generation to grow in faith and strength.

As Christian men, let us embrace our roles as protectors, nurturers, and advocates for the innocence of our youth. Together, we can ensure that our children flourish in the love of Christ, becoming beacons of hope for the world.

Defender of Childhood

EXERCISES FOR REFLECTION AND ACTION

1. Create a "Childhood Joy Jar"

Gather your family and create a "Joy Jar." Each week, write down fun memories, things that made you laugh, or moments that brought you joy. Read through the jar together at the end of each month and celebrate those moments. This exercise fosters connection and encourages gratitude.

Objective: Foster family connection and encourage gratitude by collecting and celebrating joyful memories and moments together.

	Response
	Create a Childhood Joy Jar
1.	**Memory One:**
	Description of the Joyful Moment:
	Reason for the Joyful Moment?
2.	**Memory Two:**
	Description of the Joyful Moment:
	Reason for the Joyful Moment?

51

The Christian Manhood Pledge

3.	**Memory Three:**
	Description of the Joyful Moment:
	Reason for the Joyful Moment?

2. Design a "Faith Adventure Map"

Grab some craft supplies and design a "Faith Adventure Map" together. Outline your family's spiritual journey, marking significant events like baptisms, church activities, or special prayers. Add stickers, drawings, or photos to make it vibrant. This creative project helps visualize your family's faith journey and sparks conversations about your beliefs.

Objective: Visualize your family's spiritual journey by creating a map highlighting significant faith milestones fostering conversations about beliefs and experiences.

Appendix C: Faith Adventure Map example.

Response	
Design a "Faith Adventure Map	
1.	**Significant Event One:**
	Description of the Event:
	Why Is This Event Important to Our Faith Journey?

52

2.	**Significant Event Two:**
	Description of the Event:
	Why Is This Event Important to Our Faith Journey?
3.	**Significant Event Three:**
	Description of the Event:
	Why Is This Event Important to Our Faith Journey?

3. Host a "Family Fun Day"

Plan a day dedicated to fun and connection! Organize games, outdoor activities, or a themed movie night with faith-based films. Encourage each family member to contribute ideas and make it a collaborative effort. This exercise reinforces the importance of joy in your family while nurturing bonds.

Objective: Strengthen family bonds and create joyful memories by planning a day of fun, collaborative activities that everyone can enjoy together.

The Christian Manhood Pledge

Response
Host a Family Fun Day

1.	**Activity One:**
	Description of the Activity:
	Why Is This Event Important to Our Faith Journey?
2.	**Activity Two:**
	Description of the Activity:
	Why Is This Event Important to Our Faith Journey?
3.	**Activity Three:**
	Description of the Activity:
	Why Is This Event Important to Our Faith Journey?

Defender of Childhood

4. Building a Network of Support

Plan a day dedicated to fun and connection! Organize games, outdoor activities, or a themed movie night with faith-based films. Encourage each family member to contribute ideas and make it a collaborative effort. This exercise reinforces the importance of joy in your family while nurturing bonds.

Objective: Strengthen family bonds and build a supportive Christian community by planning a day of fun and fellowship with other like-minded families. Organize activities such as group games, a potluck, or a faith-based movie night, encouraging family collaboration and connection.

	Response
	Building a Network of Support
1.	**Reflect**: Consider the relationships you currently have with other Christian families. How do these relationships influence your family's spiritual growth? Are there areas where you could strengthen or expand your support network within the Christian community?
2.	**Action**:
A.	Identify at least one Christian family or individual whose values align with yours and initiate a conversation or activity to foster deeper connections, such as sharing a meal, hosting a family Bible study, or attending a church event together.
B.	Make a plan to participate regularly in a community or church activity that encourages fellowship among Christian families, such as a men's group, small group, or a family-centered church event.
C.	Consider organizing a family-focused gathering with other Christian families, where children can play, and parents can discuss topics of faith, parenting, and support.

55

The Christian Manhood Pledge

3.	**Reflect**:

BY ACTIVELY ENGAGING IN THESE FUN AND MEANINGFUL
EXERCISES, WE CAN DEEPEN OUR COMMITMENT TO UPHOLDING
THE SANCTITY OF CHILDHOOD, CREATING LASTING MEMORIES,
AND FOSTERING A LOVING ENVIRONMENT WHERE OUR CHILDREN
CAN THRIVE.

NOTES

CHAPTER 5

HONORING AND UPLIFTING WOMEN

"Men and women are equal in worth and dignity, and when we uplift and empower women, we reflect the heart of God."
- Tony Evans.

"I renounce derogatory language against women, following the wisdom of Colossians 3:8. I pledge to honor and uplift the women of my community, as commanded in 1 Peter 3:7

Colossians 3:8 *"But now you must put them all away: anger, wrath, malice, slander, and obscene talk from your mouth."*

1 Peter 3:7 *"Likewise, husbands, live with your wives in an understanding way, showing honor to the woman as the weaker vessel, since they are heirs with you of the grace of life, so that your prayers may not be hindered."*

As Christian men, we embrace the call to demonstrate respect and honor toward women, reflecting the heart of Christ in all our interactions. This pledge to renounce derogatory language and uplift the women in our lives and communities is essential for building a foundation of love and respect. **Colossians 3:8** reminds us of the need to eliminate harmful words from our speech. At the same time, **1 Peter 3:7** emphasizes the importance of understanding and honoring the women we encounter.

The Power of Our Words

Our words hold immense power. They can build up or tear down, inspire or discourage. In a world where derogatory language can sometimes feel commonplace, it is our duty as men of faith to choose words that honor and uplift. The call to put away anger, malice, and slander is not just a personal mandate but a communal one. When we renounce harmful speech, we create an atmosphere where everyone—especially women—can thrive. The women in our lives—whether they are wives, daughters, mothers, or sisters—should feel encouraged, not belittled, by the way we speak to them and about them.

God's View on Honoring Women

God's view on how we treat others, especially women, is rooted in His creation. **Genesis 1:27** teaches us that God created both men and women in His image, making them equal in dignity and worth. Derogatory language against women dishonors God's creation and undermines the value He has placed on them. **Proverbs 31** praises the virtues of a woman, showing how much God values and honors the roles women play in His kingdom. In God's eyes, women are co-heirs to the promises of life, as **1 Peter 3:7** highlights, and are worthy of respect and honor. Any language or action that demeans women directly contradicts God's call to love our neighbors as ourselves **Matthew 22:39** and to build each other up.

The Responsibility of Leadership

Christian men are leaders within our homes, churches, and communities. This leadership is responsible for setting a standard of respect and dignity for all, especially women. The way we talk about women, even when they are not present, reveals our hearts. Are we leading by example? Our words reflect the condition of our soul, and we must allow the transformative power of Christ to shape how we communicate. Doing so requires intentionality in our speech, ensuring that our words align with the values of love, grace, and respect.

Society's View on Language and Women

Culturally, we can see a sharp contrast between how God views the treatment of women and how society views it. In today's world, derogatory language towards women is often normalized or excused in music, entertainment, and even casual conversations. Objectification and verbal disrespect are rampant, undermining women's dignity and reinforcing harmful stereotypes. However, society has also made progress by working to recognize women's rights and promote respect. While these changes show hope, real and lasting change must come from a heart transformation—something only God's love can inspire. God calls Christian men to rise above cultural standards and to be examples of Christ-like love and respect in all we do."

Living with Understanding

Understanding is essential to honoring women. **1 Peter 3:7** encourages us to live with our wives and female peers in an understanding way. Understanding includes actively listening, seeking to understand their experiences, and valuing their perspectives. When we take the time to learn from the women around us, we enrich our own lives and demonstrate genuine respect. It is not enough to refrain from derogatory language; we must also seek to engage with empathy and compassion, recognizing the unique challenges and contributions women bring to the table.

Creating a Culture of Honor

Honoring women is essential not only in our relationships but also within our communities. By promoting positive language and attitudes towards women, we help create a culture where respect is paramount. This culture benefits women and serves as an example for future generations. When young men see us treating women with honor, they learn to emulate that behavior in their own lives. In this way, we cultivate a legacy of respect that will endure beyond our lifetimes, shaping the next generation to value and uplift women in every aspect of life.

Conclusion

In this chapter, we have explored the significance of renouncing derogatory language and uplifting the women in our lives. God calls us to reflect His heart in how we treat women, knowing they are created in His image and deserving of honor. While culture may often degrade or trivialize the importance of language, we must stand firm in God's truth, rejecting societal norms that diminish the value of women. God calls Christian men to reflect Christ's love through our words and actions, creating a supportive environment for all. Committing to honor women and living with understanding can transform our communities and pave the way for a brighter future.

Let us pledge to be voices of encouragement, advocates for equality, and champions of respect. Together, we can foster a culture that uplifts and celebrates women, embodying God's love and grace.

Honoring and Uplifting Women

EXERCISES FOR REFLECTION AND ACTION

1. Positive Language Challenge

Challenge yourself to replace derogatory or harmful language with positive affirmations for one week. When you use a negative term, rephrase it into something uplifting. At the end of the week, reflect on how this change affected your interactions and the atmosphere around you.

Objective: Cultivate a more uplifting and positive communication style by replacing harmful language with affirmations and reflect on the impact this has on your interactions and environment.

Response	
Positive Language Challenge	
1.	**Negative Term Used:**
	Original Statement
	Positive Rephrase
	How did the rephrase affect the interaction?
2.	**Negative Term Used:**
	Original Statement

63

The Christian Manhood Pledge

	Positive Rephrase
	How did the rephrase affect the interaction?

2. Compliment Circle

Gather friends or family members and host a "Compliment Circle." Each person takes a turn giving genuine compliments to the women in the group. This fun exercise boosts self-esteem and reinforces the importance of uplifting language.

Objective: Boost self-esteem and reinforce the importance of uplifting language by sharing genuine compliments in a supportive group setting.

Response	
Compliment Circle	
1.	**Compliment One:**
	Compliment Given:
	Reaction of the Person Receiving the Compliment:
2.	**Compliment Two:**
	Compliment Given:

Honoring and Uplifting Women

	Reaction of the Person Receiving the Compliment:
3.	**Compliment Three:**
	Compliment Given:
	Reaction of the Person Receiving the Compliment:

3. Women's Stories Project

Objective: Honor and highlight the experiences and contributions of an inspiring woman by sharing her story and encouraging others to appreciate the value of women's voices.

Select a woman from your community or family whose story inspires you. Interview her about her experiences and insights. Create a short video or written piece to share her story, highlighting her strengths and contributions. This exercise honors her and encourages others to appreciate the value of women's voices.

Response	
Women's Stories Project	
1.	**Inspiring Woman:**
	Name of the Woman:

The Christian Manhood Pledge

Relationship to You: (e.g., family member, community leader)

Why Her Story Inspires You:

2. Inspiring Woman:

Name of the Woman:

Relationship to You: (e.g., family member, community leader)

Why Her Story Inspires You:

BY ACTIVELY PARTICIPATING IN THESE ENGAGING EXERCISES, WE CAN DEEPEN OUR COMMITMENT TO HONORING AND UPLIFTING WOMEN, CREATING A LEGACY OF RESPECT AND LOVE REFLECTING CHRIST'S HEART IN OUR COMMUNITIES.

NOTES

CHAPTER 6

HEALTH AND PURITY

"Take care of your body as if you were going to live forever; and take care of your soul as if you were going to die tomorrow."
- St. Augustine

"I vow to safeguard my body, the temple of the Holy Spirit, as instructed in 1 Corinthians 6:19-20 and 10:31, committing to glorify God in all that I do."

1 Corinthians 6:19-20: *"Or do you not know that your body is a temple of the Holy Spirit within you, whom you have from God? You are not your own, for you were bought with a price. So glorify God in your body."*

1 Corinthians 10:31:*"So, whether you eat or drink, or whatever you do, do all to the glory of God."*

As Christian men, we have a responsibility not only to our families and communities but also to ourselves. Physical health is a crucial component of our overall well-being and ability to fulfill God's calling on our lives. This chapter explores the importance of honoring our bodies through healthy living, self-care, and spiritual mindfulness.

Understanding the Importance of Physical Health

1. A Biblical Perspective:

The Bible emphasizes the value of our physical bodies as temples of the Holy Spirit. We risk limiting our capacity to serve God and others when we neglect our health. Caring for our bodies is a form of stewardship, recognizing that our health impacts our ability to live out our faith and fulfill our responsibilities.

2. The Connection Between Body and Spirit:

Physical health directly influences spiritual well-being." When we care for our bodies, we are better equipped to engage in spiritual practices, serve our communities, and be present for our families. Conversely, poor health can lead to emotional and spiritual struggles, hindering our ability to connect with God and others.

The Importance of Accountability

1. The Role of a Health Accountability Partner

A health accountability partner is vital in helping us stay committed to honoring our bodies as temples of the Holy Spirit. Whether maintaining a healthy lifestyle, attending regular doctor visits, or keeping up with spiritual disciplines, having someone to walk with us on this journey provides support and encouragement. Your accountability partner can be a family member, best friend, or colleague. Importantly, this person can be male or female—what matters is that they are someone you trust to help you stay on track with your goals. They should be willing to speak the truth in love, remind you of your commitments, and encourage you when challenges arise. In the same way, we need accountability in our spiritual walk; we also need it for our physical and emotional health.

Accountability partners help us spot areas where we may be slipping and celebrate our progress, providing encouragement and constructive feedback. Just as iron sharpens iron **Proverbs 27:17**, a trusted partner can sharpen us and help us grow stronger in our commitment to maintaining our health for God's glory.

Practical Steps to Honor Our Bodies

1. **Eat Nutritious Foods:**

Nutrition plays a significant role in our overall health. Aim to consume a balanced diet rich in fruits, vegetables, whole grains, lean proteins, and healthy fats. Mindful eating fuels our bodies and aligns with our commitment to honoring God with our choices.

2. **Stay Active:**

Regular physical activity is essential for maintaining good health. Whether playing sports, walking, or participating in workout classes, find activities you enjoy and make them a regular part of your routine. Physical exercise benefits your body and enhances your mental and emotional well-being.

3. **Prioritize Rest:**

Adequate rest and sleep are vital for maintaining health and functioning effectively. In our busy lives, it can be tempting to sacrifice rest, but doing so can lead to burnout and health issues. Prioritize quality sleep and take breaks to recharge your mind and body.

4. **Stay Hydrated:**

Drinking enough water is crucial for physical health. Aim to drink plenty of water throughout the day to stay hydrated and support your body's functions. Proper hydration can enhance your energy levels and concentration, making engaging in your daily responsibilities easier.

The Role of Mental and Emotional Health

1. **Practice Mindfulness:**

Mental and emotional well-being is as important as physical health. Engage in mindfulness practices, such as meditation or prayer, to cultivate inner peace and reduce stress. Take time each day to reflect on your thoughts and feelings, seeking God's guidance in your mental health journey.

2. **Build Supportive Relationships:**

Surround yourself with supportive friends and family who encourage your health and well-being. Engage in open conversations about mental health and seek support when needed. Vulnerability and connection with others are essential for maintaining emotional health.

3. **Seek Professional Help:**

If you struggle with mental health issues, do not hesitate to seek professional help. Therapy and counseling can provide valuable tools for managing stress, anxiety, and depression. Recognizing when to ask for help is a sign of strength, not weakness.

Honoring Our Bodies Through Spiritual Practices

1. **Daily Prayer and Reflection**: One of the most powerful ways to honor your body is through consistent prayer and reflection. Begin each day by asking God for strength and guidance to make healthy choices that glorify Him. Spend time reflecting on Scriptures, like **1 Corinthians 6:19-20**, that remind you of the sacredness of your body as a temple of the Holy Spirit. Praying for wisdom in maintaining physical and mental health reinforces your commitment to living according to God's will.

2. **Fasting and Spiritual Discipline**: We can use fasting, a biblical practice, to discipline the body and focus on spiritual growth. Setting aside time to fast—from food or other distractions—you can deepen your connection to God and practice self-control. Jesus fasted for 40 days in the wilderness **Matthew 4:2**, setting an example of how we can discipline our bodies in pursuit of spiritual clarity and strength. Fasting can help reset your physical and spiritual priorities, aligning them with God's purposes.

3. **Incorporate Worship into Movement**: Engage in physical activities that nourish your soul, such as walking or running while meditating on Scripture or listening to worship music. Turn exercise into a form of worship by dedicating your movement to God and focusing your heart and mind on Him throughout the process. As you strengthen your body, you can also draw closer to God, making your fitness routine a holistic practice that feeds both body and spirit.

4. **Rest and Sabbath**: Observing the Sabbath and prioritizing rest is essential for spiritual and physical well-being. God commands us to rest, as He rested on the

seventh day after creation **Genesis 2:2-3.** By intentionally setting aside time for rest and renewal, you honor God and allow your body to rejuvenate. The Sabbath is a time to refresh physically, reflect on God's goodness, and refocus spiritually.

5. **Gratitude and Stewardship**: Cultivate a mindset of appreciation for the body God has given you. Each day, thank God for the health and abilities you possess, no matter your limitations. Viewing your health as a gift from God fosters an attitude of stewardship. Caring for your body—through nutrition, exercise, rest, and mental health practices—becomes an act of worship, showing gratitude to God for the gift of life and health.

Conclusion

Honoring our bodies is not just a responsibility but a sacred act of Christian manhood. By prioritizing our physical, mental, and emotional health, we become better equipped to fulfill the God-given duties entrusted to us in our families and communities. Our health is not isolated—it profoundly impacts our ability to serve others and live out our faith effectively.

As Christian men, let us commit to treating our bodies as temples of the Holy Spirit, making deliberate and mindful choices that reflect our devotion to God. By striving for better health, we gain the energy and clarity to engage more deeply in our relationships and positively influence those around us.

Recognizing that our physical health is vital to our spiritual journey enables us to live out our purpose fully. By honoring our bodies, we glorify God in all we do and set an example for others, becoming vessels of strength, service, and love in every area of life.

The Christian Manhood Pledge

EXERCISES FOR REFLECTION AND ACTION

1. Healthy Cooking Challenge

Gather your family or friends and host a "Healthy Cooking Challenge." Each participant can prepare a nutritious dish using wholesome ingredients. Set a theme, such as "Colorful Plates" (focus on fruits and vegetables) or "Lean and Green" (lean proteins and greens). After cooking, everyone can share their dish and discuss the health benefits of their ingredients. Not only is this a fun way to encourage healthy eating, but it also fosters community and creativity in the kitchen.

Objective: Encourage healthy eating habits and foster community and creativity by preparing and sharing nutritious dishes with family or friends.

Response	
Healthy Cooking Challenge	
1.	**Dish One:**
	Name of the Dish:
	Theme: (e.g., "Colorful Plates," "Lean and Green")
	Key Ingredients Used:

74

Health and Purity

Health Benefits of the Ingredients:

| 2. | Dish Two: |
| | Name of the Dish: |

Theme: (e.g., "Colorful Plates," "Lean and Green")

Key Ingredients Used:

Health Benefits of the Ingredients:

| 3. | Dish Three |
| | Name of the Dish: |

Theme: (e.g., "Colorful Plates," "Lean and Green")
Key Ingredients Used:
Health Benefits of the Ingredients:

2. Movement Adventure

Create a "Movement Adventure" day where you try out different physical activities. Choose three or four activities (e.g., hiking, biking, dancing, or playing a sport) and engage in each. You can invite friends or family to join, turning it into a friendly competition or a fun day out. Afterward, discuss which activities everyone enjoyed the most and how they made you feel physically and mentally.

Objective: Promote physical well-being and strengthen bonds by exploring various physical activities with friends or family, reflecting on the impact on both body and mind.

Response	
Movement Adventure	
1.	**Activity One:**
	Name of the Activity: (e.g., Hiking, Biking)
	Participants:

Health and Purity

How the Activity Made You Feel Physically:

How the Activity Made You Feel Mentally:

2. | **Activity Two:**

Name of the Activity: (e.g., Hiking, Biking)

Participants:

How the Activity Made You Feel Physically:

How the Activity Made You Feel Mentally:

3. | **Activity Three:**

Name of the Activity: (e.g., Hiking, Biking)

Participants:

How the Activity Made You Feel Physically:

How the Activity Made You Feel Mentally:

The Christian Manhood Pledge

3. Mindfulness Minute

Designate a "Mindfulness Minute" each day for one week. During this minute, find a quiet space to practice mindfulness through prayer, meditation, or deep breathing exercises. You can even create a visual cue, like a colorful reminder on your phone or a sticky note on your mirror, to help you remember. At the end of the week, reflect on how taking this time impacted your mental and emotional well-being.

Objective: Enhance mental and emotional well-being by practicing daily mindfulness through prayer, meditation, or deep breathing and reflecting on its impact over a week.

Response
Mindfulness Minute
1. **Day One:**
Mindfulness Practice: (e.g., Prayer, Meditation, Deep Breathing)
How It Made You Feel Mentally:
How It Made You Feel Emotionally:

78

Health and Purity

2.	**Day Two:**

Mindfulness Practice (e.g., Prayer, Meditation, Deep Breathing):

How It Made You Feel Mentally:

How It Made You Feel Emotionally:

3.	**Day Three:**

Mindfulness Practice (e.g., Prayer, Meditation, Deep Breathing):

How It Made You Feel Mentally:

The Christian Manhood Pledge

How It Made You Feel Emotionally:

4. Day Four:

Mindfulness Practice (e.g., Prayer, Meditation, Deep Breathing):

How It Made You Feel Mentally:

How It Made You Feel Emotionally:

5. Day Five:

Mindfulness Practice (e.g., Prayer, Meditation, Deep Breathing):

How It Made You Feel Mentally:

How It Made You Feel Emotionally:

6. Day Six:

Mindfulness Practice (e.g., Prayer, Meditation, Deep Breathing):

How It Made You Feel Mentally:

How It Made You Feel Emotionally:

The Christian Manhood Pledge

7.	**Day Seven:**

Mindfulness Practice (e.g., Prayer, Meditation, Deep Breathing):

How It Made You Feel Mentally:

How It Made You Feel Emotionally:

BY ACTIVELY ENGAGING IN THESE FUN AND REFLECTIVE EXERCISES, WE CAN DEEPEN OUR COMMITMENT TO HONORING OUR BODIES AND NURTURING OUR OVERALL WELL-BEING. EACH EXERCISE ENCOURAGES PERSONAL GROWTH AND CONNECTION WITH OTHERS, REINFORCING THE IMPORTANCE OF COMMUNITY IN OUR HEALTH JOURNEY.

NOTES

CHAPTER 7

COMMUNITY SUPPORT AND UNITY

"Life's most persistent and urgent question is, 'What are you doing for others?"
-Martin Luther King Jr.

"I commit to supporting and uplifting my community with unwavering dedication, inspired by Romans 15:2 and Philippians 2:4, striving to promote positivity and unity."

Romans 15:2: *"Let each of us please his neighbor for his good, to build him up."*

Philippians 2:4: *"Let each of you look not only to his own interests, but also to the interests of others."*

God calls Christian men to actively engage with their communities, serving others and contributing to the common good. This chapter explores the significance of community involvement, the biblical foundation for serving others, and practical ways to impact our neighborhoods positively and beyond.

The Biblical Call to Community Engagement

1. **A Reflection of Christ's Love:** Jesus modeled a life of service throughout His ministry. He engaged with the marginalized, healed the sick, fed the hungry, and taught His followers to love their neighbors. Our call to serve others reflects Christ's love and an expression of our faith. In serving our communities, we demonstrate the heart of God and fulfill His command to love one another.

2. **The Body of Christ:** In **1 Corinthians 12:12-14**, Paul describes the church as the body of Christ, with each member playing a vital role. Engaging with our community allows us to contribute our unique gifts and talents to benefit the whole body. When we serve, we help strengthen and support the community of believers and those outside the church.

3. **Promoting Justice and Mercy: Micah 6:8** calls us to *"do justice, love kindness, and walk humbly with your God."* Engaging with our communities involves advocating for justice, mercy, and compassion. God calls us to advocate for those who cannot advocate for themselves and to strive for a society that embodies His values of love and justice.

Practical Ways to Serve Our Communities

1. **Volunteer Locally:** Seek out local organizations, charities, or churches that need volunteers. Whether serving at a food bank, tutoring children, or participating in community clean-up days, volunteering is a tangible way to impact your community positively. Encourage your family to join you in these efforts, creating shared experiences and fostering a spirit of service.

2. **Support Local Businesses:** Engage with and support local businesses within your community. By shopping locally, you contribute to the economic well-being of your neighborhood and help create jobs for others. Take the time to build relationships with business owners and encourage others to do the same.

3. **Participate in Community Events:** Attend and participate in local events, such as fairs, festivals, or town hall meetings. Being present in your community helps you stay informed about local issues and provides opportunities to connect with others and build relationships. Use these gatherings to share your faith and witness to others.

4. **Offer Your Skills:** Use your talents and skills to serve others in your community. Whether you are a mechanic, teacher, artist, or tradesman, consider offering your services for free or at a reduced rate to those in need. Sharing your expertise can be a powerful way to bless others while building connections within your community.

5. **Mentor Others:** Train young people or those in your community who may benefit from your guidance. Whether through formal programs or informal relationships, mentorship can have a lasting impact on someone's life. Please share your experiences, offer encouragement, and help them develop their skills and talents.

Building Relationships and Community

1. **Foster Relationships:** Building genuine relationships within your community is essential for effective service. Take the time to get to know your neighbors, listen to their stories, and understand their needs. Strong relationships provide a foundation for meaningful service and foster a sense of belonging.

2. **Create a Support Network:** Establish a support network within your community that encourages collaboration and mutual aid. Work together with others to address everyday needs, share resources, and support one another. This network can amplify your impact and create a culture of care and generosity.

3. **Pray for Your Community:** Commit to praying for your community regularly. Seek God's guidance for its issues and ask for wisdom in how to serve effectively. Prayer invites God into your efforts and aligns your heart with His purpose for the community.

The Impact of Community Engagement

1. **Transforming Lives:** Engaging with our communities can transform our lives and those we serve. By sharing our time, resources, and love, we can make a difference in the lives of individuals and families. Each act of service contributes to a larger narrative of hope and healing.

2. **Building God's Kingdom:** When we engage with our communities, we build God's kingdom on earth. Our actions reflect His love and grace, drawing others to Him. As we serve, we create opportunities for spiritual conversations and witness, allowing others to experience the transformative power of Christ.

3. **Leaving a Legacy:** Community engagement helps us leave a legacy of faith and service for future generations. When we model active engagement and selfless service, we inspire those around us—especially our children—to do the same. Our commitment to serving others creates a ripple effect beyond our immediate actions.

Conclusion

Engaging with our communities is an essential aspect of Christian manhood that reflects our faith and commitment to serving others. By actively participating in our neighborhoods and investing in the lives of those around us, we fulfill our calling to love our neighbors and contribute to the common good.

Let us commit to engaging in our communities with open hearts and hands, seeking opportunities to serve and uplift those in need. As we embody the love of Christ through our actions, we can make a lasting impact that extends beyond our lives and glorifies God.

May we remember that our community engagement is not just an obligation but a joyful expression of our faith. Through service, we become vessels of God's love, hope, and grace, transforming lives and building a better world for His glory.

Community Support and Unity

EXERCISES FOR REFLECTION AND ACTION

1. Community Mapping

Gather a group of friends or family and create a large map of your community on a poster board or digitally using mapping software.

Identify critical locations: schools, parks, local businesses, churches, and community centers.

Discuss and mark areas where you see needs (e.g., a local park that needs cleanup, a school that could use tutoring volunteers) and strengths (e.g., thriving local businesses, active community groups).

Reflect on how you can contribute to addressing these needs and enhancing strengths. Choose one area to focus on for your next community engagement activity.

Objective: Identify the needs and strengths of your community.

See Appendix D: Community Mapping Example: Fictitious Community – Oakwood Village

Response
Community Mapping
1.   **Critical Location One:**
Name and Description of the Location: (e.g., Local Park, School)
Identified Needs:

89

The Christian Manhood Pledge

| Identified Strengths: |
| |
| |
| |
| How We Can Contribute: |
| |
| |
| |

2. Critical Location Two:

Name and Description of the Location: (e.g., Local Park, School)

| |
| |
| |
| Identified Needs: |
| |
| |
| |
| Identified Strengths: |
| |
| |
| |
| How We Can Contribute: |
| |
| |
| |

3. Critical Location Three:

Name and Description of the Location: (e.g., Local Park, School)

| |
| |
| |
| Identified Needs: |
| |

Community Support and Unity

Identified Strengths:
How We Can Contribute:

2. Storytelling and Sharing

Organize a small gathering with friends, family, or community members. Choose a theme related to community engagement (e.g., "A time I was helped by someone in my community" or "A time I made a difference in someone else's life").

Each person takes turns sharing their story, focusing on the impact of community support and engagement.

After everyone shares, discuss how these stories inspire you to take action in your community. Create a collective list of ideas for community projects or initiatives inspired by the stories.

Objective: Foster connection through personal stories and experiences.

Response	
Storytelling and Sharing	
1.	**Story One:**
Theme: (e.g., "A time I was helped by someone in my community")	

The Christian Manhood Pledge

Summary of the Story:

Impact of the Story on the Community or Individual:

Inspiration for Future Action:

2.	**Story Two:**

Theme: (e.g., "A time I made a difference in someone else's life)

Summary of the Story:

Impact of the Story on the Community or Individual:

Inspiration for Future Action:

Community Support and Unity

3. Service Vision Board

A **Community Service Vision Board** is a powerful tool to visualize your goals, stay motivated, and remind yourself why service is essential. It helps you organize your ideas and inspires you daily to act and make a difference in your community.

Objective: Visualize and commit to your community engagement goals.

Appendix E: Example of a "Service Vision Board and Step By Step Instructions"

Response	
Service Vision Board	
1.	**Passions and Skills:**
What are your passions?	
What skills do you have to offer?	
2.	**Identified Community Needs:**
What needs have you identified in your community?	

93

The Christian Manhood Pledge

How can your passions and skills help address these needs?

3. Vision Board Elements:

Images and Words Included:

Quotes or Inspirational Phrases:

Overall Theme or Focus of Your Vision Board:

Inspiration for Future Action:

4. Commitment and Timeline:

What specific actions will you take toward your goals?

Community Support and Unity

Timeline for Taking Action:
Accountability Partner (if applicable):

THESE EXERCISES PROMOTE MEANINGFUL ENGAGEMENT AND ENCOURAGE REFLECTION, COLLABORATION, AND ACTIONABLE COMMITMENT TO SERVING YOUR COMMUNITY. PARTICIPATING IN THESE ACTIVITIES CAN STRENGTHEN YOUR CONNECTIONS AND DEEPEN YOUR IMPACT ON THOSE AROUND YOU.

NOTES

CHAPTER 8

DIVINE STRENGTH AND GUIDANCE

"Without the Spirit of God, we can do nothing.
We are as ships without wind. We are useless."
- **Charles Spurgeon.**

"In making these pledges, I seek the strength and guidance of Almighty God, acknowledging that my own power can accomplish none of this. As stated in Philippians 4:13, 'I can do all things through Him who strengthens me.' This declaration is a statement of intent and a prayer for endurance, wisdom, and courage to live out these commitments. So help me God."

Philippians 4:13: "I can do all things through him who strengthens me."

In this final chapter, we reflect on the importance of seeking God's strength and guidance in every aspect of our lives. As Christian men, we recognize that our abilities and efforts are rooted in our relationship with Him. By pledging to rely on His power, we can pursue our calling with confidence and purpose, knowing we are never alone.

Seeking God's Strength

1. The Source of Our Strength

Philippians 4:13 reminds us, *"I can do all things through him who strengthens me."* This powerful verse emphasizes that our strength does not come from ourselves but from our relationship with Christ. We acknowledge our dependence on Him daily and open ourselves to His guidance and empowerment.

2. Embracing God's Guidance

As we embark on various endeavors—whether in our families, careers, or communities—it is essential to seek God's wisdom and direction. Prayer and reflection on His Word allow us to align our goals with His purposes, ensuring that our actions reflect His will.

3. Trusting in His Provision

God equips us with the resources we need to fulfill our callings. When we trust in His provision, we can confidently take steps forward, even facing challenges. Our faith empowers us to step out of our comfort zones and embrace the opportunities He places before us.

Conclusion:

A Call to Salvation and Sanctification

As we conclude this journey through *The Christian Manhood Pledge*, let us remember that our commitment to God is not merely a set of promises but a heartfelt dedication to living in His strength and purpose. We can impact our families, communities, and the world by seeking His guidance and relying on His power.

The journey of Christian manhood begins with a personal relationship with Jesus Christ. To those who have never surrendered their life to Christ or have drifted from their faith, this is an invitation to begin anew. The path toward true manhood, as explored in *The Christian Manhood Pledge*, starts and ends with Jesus. No commitment, pledge, or promise holds its entire meaning without first giving your life to Him. Only through this surrender can you truly embrace the purpose, strength, and integrity that God has intended for you, stepping fully into the calling of a Christian man.

The Bible offers us a clear path to salvation, called the **Romans Road to Salvation**. This series of key verses from the Book of Romans provides a roadmap for understanding humanity's need for salvation and God's provision through Jesus Christ. **Romans 10:9** *"Because, if you confess with your mouth that Jesus is Lord and believe in your heart that God raised him from the dead, you will be saved."* This is the foundation of the Christian faith—acknowledging Jesus Christ as Lord and believing in His resurrection.

The Romans Road to Salvation

To further explain the path to salvation, reflect on these critical verses from the Book of Romans:

1. **Romans 3:23** – *"For all have sinned and fall short of the glory of God."*
2. **Romans 6:23** – *"For the wages of sin is death, but the free gift of God is eternal life in Christ Jesus our Lord."*
3. **Romans 5:8** – *"But God shows his love for us in that while we were still sinners, Christ died for us."*
4. **Romans 10:9-10** – *"Because, if you confess with your mouth that Jesus is Lord and believe in your heart that God raised him from the dead, you will be saved. For with the heart one believes and is justified, and with the mouth one confesses and is saved."*
5. **Romans 10:13** – *"For everyone who calls on the name of the Lord will be saved."*

For Those Who Have Never Given Their Life to Christ:

If you've never made this decision, I encourage you to take this step today. It is the most important decision you will ever make. To accept Christ as your Savior, pray a prayer like this from your heart:

Lord Jesus, I acknowledge that I am a sinner in need of Your grace. I believe that You died for my sins and that God raised You from the dead. I confess that You are Lord of my life. Come into my heart and make me a new creation. Thank You for saving me. In Your name, I pray. Amen.

If you've just prayed this prayer, welcome to the family of God! You are beginning a new life in Christ, fully equipped to live out the Christian manhood we've discussed throughout this book.

For Those Who Have Backslidden:

For those who once walked with Christ but have drifted away, know that God's arms are always open, ready to welcome you back. Christ's love never fails, and His mercy renews every morning. Just as the prodigal son's father welcomed him back, our Heavenly Father will welcome you, too.

Pray this prayer to rededicate your life to Christ:

Lord, I confess that I have strayed from Your path. I ask for Your forgiveness and grace to return to You. I believe that Your sacrifice on the cross covers all my sins, and I recommit my life to You. Renew my heart and lead me in Your ways. Thank You for Your endless love and mercy. In Jesus' name, I pray. Amen.

As you recommit your life to Christ, remember that His grace is sufficient for you. No matter where you've been or what you've done, His love can restore you.

Understanding Sanctification:

The journey doesn't end there once you have accepted Christ as your Savior or recommitted your life to Him. It's just the beginning. The Bible speaks of sanctification, which is the process of being made holy and growing in spiritual maturity. Sanctification is God's ongoing work, transforming us daily to be more like Christ.

This process involves renewing your mind, heart, and actions as you submit to God's will and allow the Holy Spirit to guide you. It's a lifelong journey that requires dedication, prayer, studying God's Word, and living out your faith daily. As you grow in your relationship with God, you will see the fruits of the Spirit—love, joy, peace, patience, kindness, goodness, faithfulness, gentleness, and self-control—manifesting in your life **Galatians 5:22-23**.

The Importance of Belonging to a Church Community:

The journey of sanctification is not one to walk alone. God designed us to live in community with other believers, which is why being part of a church is essential. The church is not just a building; it is the living body of Christ, composed of individuals who support, encourage, and hold one another accountable in their walk with God. In this community, we find strength, wisdom, and fellowship, equipping us to grow in faith and deepen our commitment to Christ.

Belonging to a church provides spiritual growth, fellowship, accountability, service opportunities, and corporate worship. As you continue your faith journey, I encourage you to find a local church where you can belong, grow, and serve.

A Note About Seeking a Church

As you continue your faith journey, finding a church that aligns with your spiritual needs and supports your growth is crucial. There are generally two types of churches: organizational and organic (or organism).

The organizational church often focuses on structure, legalism, and maintaining itself as an institution. We can categorize it into three types:"

Legalistic churches: These churches may emphasize strict adherence to rules, rituals, and traditions, often focusing more on the letter of the law than on the spirit of the gospel.

Containment churches are inward-focused, often open only during specific hours and rarely engaging with the broader community. Their primary concern is maintaining stability within their walls rather than ministering to the world outside.

Entertainment churches: Here, the focus is more on attracting people through performance and spectacle. While these churches may draw large crowds, they may sometimes lack discipleship or depth of spiritual formation.

While organizational churches can offer straightforward programs and resources, they can also become more about maintaining systems and traditions than truly ministering to people.

The organism church, on the other hand, functions as the living, breathing body of Christ—ministering as Jesus did. Jesus modeled this in His ministry, where He gathered in homes, marketplaces, and the streets, ministering to the needs of the people. In **Matthew 18:20**, He says, *"For where two or three are gathered in my name, there am I among them."* This church is less about buildings or structures and more about the people, the relationships, and the authentic experience of following Christ together.

In the organism church, believers are encouraged to live out their faith in genuine community, holding each other accountable, serving one another, and engaging with the world around them. This type of church focuses on spiritual growth, personal transformation, and bringing Christ's love to the community. I encourage you to seek a church like this, where you can experience true fellowship and actively participate in ministry as Jesus intended.

On this side of Glory, you won't find a perfect church.

There's an old saying that "if you find a perfect church, it becomes imperfect the moment you join." This reality highlights that imperfect people make up churches. The goal is not perfection but finding a community where you can grow in your relationship with Christ, serve others, and live out your commitments in *The Christian Manhood Pledge*. Surround yourself with godly men who will walk alongside you on this journey. Whether in an organizational or organism church, the body of Christ is a family that supports spiritual growth, accountability, and service.

Becoming a Disciple: The Call to Make Disciples of Others

After completing *The Christian Manhood Pledge*, you are equipped to live a life of integrity and purpose and called to disciple others. Jesus' final command to His followers, known as the Great Commission, challenges us to go out and make disciples of all nations:

"Go therefore and make disciples of all nations, baptizing them in the name of the Father, Son, and the Holy Spirit, teaching them to observe all that I have commanded you. And behold, I am with you always, to the end of the age" **Matthew 28:19-20**.

After completing *The Christian Manhood Pledge*, you are equipped to live a life of integrity and purpose and are called to disciple others. Jesus' final command to His followers, known as the Great Commission, challenges us to go out and make disciples of all nations:

"Go therefore and make disciples of all nations, baptizing them in the name of the Father, Son, and the Holy Spirit, teaching them to observe all that I have commanded you. And behold, I am with you always, to the end of the age" **Matthew 28:19-20**.

You are embarking on a journey of Christian manhood—a lifelong commitment to sharing the Gospel and investing in the spiritual growth of others. As you grow in your faith, God can use your journey and the lessons in *The Christian Manhood Pledge* to disciple men, women, and even children. Whether through mentorship, teaching, or simply living out the principles of this pledge, God calls you to guide others on their path toward Christian maturity. Your life becomes a powerful example of what it means to walk with Christ.

This book serves as an essential tool in your discipleship journey. Use its teachings and pledges to foster conversations, promote accountability, and create a framework for spiritual growth. Now is the time to take what you've learned and help others build a solid foundation of faith, teaching them to honor God in all areas of their lives, just as you have committed to doing.

As you continue your journey, remember that discipleship is not about perfection but walking alongside others, sharing their struggles, and helping them grow in their relationship with Christ. Just as Jesus walked with His disciples, God calls you to walk with others, helping them live out their faith and fulfill their God-given purpose.

The Christian Manhood Pledge

Divine Strength and Guidance

As we conclude *The Christian Manhood Pledge*, reflecting on the foundational truth that we do not walk this journey alone is essential. Our strength and wisdom come from God, who sustains us through His Spirit. As Charles Spurgeon reminds us, "Without the Spirit of God, we can do nothing. We are as ships without wind. We are useless." This divine truth underscores the critical role of God's strength in all we do.

Philippians 4:13 reinforces this: *"I can do all things through Him who strengthens me."* We must constantly seek God's strength, acknowledging that our abilities are insufficient for the tasks ahead. As we make our pledges and strive to live out the commitments of Christian manhood, His guidance and power enable us to stand firm. We are not simply working for ourselves or our families; we are laboring for the Kingdom of God, which requires divine empowerment.

As we seek God's strength and guidance, He reminds us to humble ourselves and seek His will daily. As Christian men, we root our purpose not in worldly success or personal accolades but in fulfilling God's call in our lives with integrity and faith. Fulfilling this purpose requires a daily surrender to His will, trusting Him in our successes and struggles. His strength is made perfect in our weakness **2 Corinthians 12:9**, and through Him, we can overcome every obstacle, fulfill our roles, and live out our commitments.

Final Charge

Let us go forth, empowered by His strength, confident in His guidance, and dedicated to fulfilling our purpose for His glory. As men of faith, integrity, and service, may we fully engage in God's calling on our lives. Together, let us be a force for transformation, impacting our families, communities, and the world for Christ.

God calls us to be more than mere participants in life—He calls us to lead, serve, and be beacons of light in a dark world. Answering this call means stepping out in faith, even when the path is uncertain, and trusting His strength and wisdom will guide us. As we commit ourselves to honor Him in every aspect of our lives—whether in our work, relationships, or spiritual growth—we have the assurance that God will equip us for the journey ahead.

May we also recognize that the transformation God brings through us is not limited to ourselves. As we grow in faith and character, we strengthen our families, build up our communities, and spread the love and truth of Christ throughout our world. God calls us salt and light **Matthew 5:13-16**, preserving what is good and shining brightly in the darkness—not by our might but by the power of the Holy Spirit.

Therefore, let us commit to living lives of purpose, driven by divine strength and guided by His wisdom. Let us encourage one another in brotherhood, walking side by side as we pursue the high calling of Christ. Together, we can be agents of transformation, standing as men of God, ready to fulfill our mission for His Kingdom and His glory.

As we conclude *The Christian Manhood Pledge*, let it not simply be words recited but a living declaration of our commitment to God and His purpose for our lives. This pledge is a call to action—an unwavering dedication to embodying the principles of faith, integrity, responsibility, and service. By embracing this pledge, we declare that we are men who will honor our bodies as temples of the Holy Spirit, lead our families with love and wisdom, serve our communities with humility, and stand boldly for Christ in a world that desperately needs His light.

With the strength and guidance of Almighty God, we can live out these commitments each day, confident that *'He who began a good work in you will be faithful to complete it'* **Philippians 1:6**. May this pledge serve as a continual reminder of our purpose, empowering us to lead, serve, and grow as men of faith. Together, let us continue, pledging to be living examples of Christ's love and leadership in all we do. So help us, God.

The Christian Manhood Pledge

EXERCISES FOR REFLECTION AND ACTION

1. Strength Inventory

A. Take a quiet moment to reflect on different aspects of your life (e.g., family, work, relationships, personal growth)

B. In each row, write down one aspect of your life, the challenges you face, and how you can seek God's strength (e.g., through prayer, Scripture, or seeking counsel).

C. **Share your inventory with your accountability partner** for support and mutual growth. You invite accountability and encouragement into your journey by openly discussing your goals, challenges, and progress.

Objective: Identify areas where you can rely more on God's strength.

Response	
Strength Inventory	
1.	**Aspect of Life One:**
Current Challenges:	
Ways to Rely on God's Strength:	

Divine Strength and Guidance

2.   Aspect of Life Two:

Current Challenges:

Ways to Rely on God's Strength:

3.   Aspect of Life Three:

Current Challenges:

Ways to Rely on God's Strength:

4.   Aspect of Life Four:

Current Challenges:

Ways to Rely on God's Strength:

2. Prayer Walk

A. Plan a "Prayer Walk" in your neighborhood or a nearby park. Take your accountability partner, a friend, or a family member with you.

B. As you walk, pray for the people, families, and places you see. Ask God to reveal how you can serve and engage with your community.

C. Take note of specific areas or needs that resonate with you. Based on what you observed during your walk, consider ways to actively support and uplift those in your community.

Objective: Seek God's guidance through prayer while engaging with your community.

Response
Prayer Walk
1.   **Location One:**
Description of the Place: (e.g., Neighborhood, Park)
Prayer Focus: (People, Families, Specific Needs)
Observations/Resonating Needs:
Ideas for Support/Engagement:

Divine Strength and Guidance

2.	**Location Two:**
Description of the Place: (e.g., Neighborhood, Park)	
Prayer Focus: (People, Families, Specific Needs)	
Observations/Resonating Needs:	
Ideas for Support/Engagement:	

3. Stepping Out in Faith

Identify one area of your life (e.g., family, career, or service) where you feel God is calling you to step out of your comfort zone. It could be taking on a new role at church, starting a new project, or helping someone in need. Pray for courage and take that step of faith, trusting in God's provision.

Objective: Trust God's provision and take steps of faith in an area where you feel called.

Response	
Stepping Out in Faith	
1.	**Step of Faith**
Describe the step of faith taken.	

109

2.	How You Felt Before:
Initial feelings of doubt, fear, or excitement:	

3.	How You Felt During:
Emotions and thoughts as you took the action:	

4.	How You Felt After:
Reflect on your emotions after completing the step:	

5.	How You Saw God's Provision:
What evidence or signs did you see of God's provision?	

4. Awakening the Warrior Within

This exercise, "Awakening the Warrior Within," provides a structured approach for Christian men to embrace their spiritual role as warriors. It uses biblical references, reflection, and practical steps to help participants grow in faith and strength.

Objective: This exercise helps Christian men awaken the inner warrior—one who stands firm in the faith, defends truth, protects the vulnerable, and fights spiritual battles with integrity and strength. By reflecting on Scripture and taking practical actions, participants will be encouraged to embrace their daily role as warriors for Christ.

Divine Strength and Guidance

Response
Awakening The Warrior Within

Step 1.	**Reflect on Your Identity as a Warrior**

Read:

Ephesians 6:10-18 – The Armor of God.

2 Timothy 2:3-4 – Endure hardship like a good soldier of Christ.

1 Corinthians 16:13-14 – Be watchful, stand firm in the faith, be courageous, be strong.

Journal Questions:

1. What does it mean to be a spiritual warrior in the context of my faith?

2. How do these scriptures challenge me to take up my role as a protector, leader, and fighter for righteousness?

3. In what areas of my life am I called to "stand firm" and defend truth or justice?

The Christian Manhood Pledge

Step 2.	Gear Up with the Armor of God

Action:

Take a moment to visualize yourself putting on the armor of God (Ephesians 6:10-18). For each piece, reflect on how you can apply it to your life today:

1.	Belt of Truth: How can I live out the truth in my speech, actions, and thoughts today?

2.	Breastplate of Righteousness: What area of my life needs greater alignment with God's standards?

3.	Feet Fitted with the Gospel of Peace: Who in my life needs to experience the peace of Christ?

4.	Shield of Faith: What challenge must I face with unwavering faith?

5.	Helmet of Salvation: How does my identity in Christ give me courage and strength today?

112

6.	Sword of the Spirit (God's Word): What Scripture can I use today as a weapon in my spiritual battles?

Step 3.	**Face Your Battles**

Personal Battle Plan:

Identify three spiritual, emotional, or physical battles you are currently facing. Write them down

1.	Spiritual

2.	Emotional

3.	Physical

Prayer:	Surrender these battles to God in prayer, asking for His strength to face them as a warrior of Christ.

The Christian Manhood Pledge

Strategy:	For each battle, write down one Scripture and one action you will take to fight this battle with integrity, faith, and courage.

Step 4.	**Commit to Defending the Vulnerable**

Read:

Proverbs 31:8-9 – Speak up for those who cannot speak for themselves.

1 Peter 3:7 – Honor women and treat them with respect.

1 Corinthians 16:13-14 – Be watchful, stand firm in the faith, be courageous, be strong.

Action:

1. Identify someone in your life or community who is vulnerable (whether emotionally, spiritually, or physically). It could be a family member, friend, or even a social issue that needs attention.

Divine Strength and Guidance

2.	Write down a practical action you can take this week to defend, support, or uplift this person or cause, whether through encouragement, prayer, service, or standing up for justice.

Step 5.	Make a Warrior's Covenant

Commitment Prayer:

Take time to pray and make a personal covenant with God, asking Him to awaken the warrior in you. Acknowledge your role as a warrior of faith, and commit to standing firm in His truth, protecting those in need, and fighting spiritual battles with courage.

Lord, awaken the warrior in me. I commit to standing firm in Your truth, defending those who cannot protect themselves, and fighting my battles with faith, courage, and integrity. Equip me with Your armor and guide me as I fulfill my role as a warrior for Your kingdom. Amen.

Challenge:

Share this exercise with an accountability partner. Discuss how you can stay committed to living out your roles as Christian warriors. Consider checking in weekly to share your progress and offer encouragement.

By consistently practicing these steps, you will awaken the warrior within and become a stronger defender of faith, family, and righteousness.

THESE EXERCISES FOSTER INTENTIONAL REFLECTION AND PURPOSEFUL ACTION, ENCOURAGING PARTICIPANTS TO DEEPEN THEIR RELIANCE ON GOD'S STRENGTH, WISDOM, AND PROVISION. ENGAGING IN THESE ACTIVITIES HELPS CHRISTIAN MEN ALIGN THEIR LIVES WITH HIS WILL, STEP OUT IN FAITH, AND POSITIVELY IMPACT THOSE AROUND THEM. THROUGH THESE REFLECTIVE PRACTICES, MEN CAN STRENGTHEN THEIR RELATIONSHIP WITH GOD AND EXTEND HIS LOVE TO THEIR FAMILIES AND COMMUNITIES.

NOTES

CHAPTER 9

FINAL STEP

"God is more interested in your faithfulness than your success. Finish well, and leave the results to Him."
— **Rick Warren**

"I have fought the good fight, I have finished the race, I have kept the faith."
2 Timothy 4:7

Formalizing Your Commitment

As you have journeyed through *The Christian Manhood Pledge*, you have reflected deeply on your role as a man of faith and committed to living out the principles God has called you to. Each chapter has guided you through self-examination, prayer, and action, rooted in a desire to grow in your walk with Christ.

Now, as you reach the culmination of this journey, it's time to take a tangible step to formalize your commitment.

The Christian Manhood Pledge

Post-Evaluation: Confidence After Completing the Pledges

Instructions:

After completing the book and engaging with each pledge, revisit this table to evaluate your growth in confidence. For each pledge, **circle the scale** that best reflects your current confidence in fulfilling that pledge.

Scale		
1	**Struggling**	I have little to no knowledge or experience; it's a challenge for me.
2	**Building**	I have some knowledge but still need help to improve.
3	**Developing**	I have a good foundation and am growing; there's still more to learn.
4	**Strong**	I am confident and knowledgeable in fulfilling this pledge.

Pledges	Confidence Level			
Love and Devotion	1	2	3	4
Diligence and Prosperity	1	2	3	4
Protection and Love	1	2	3	4
Defender of Childhood	1	2	3	4
Honoring and Uplifting Women	1	2	3	4
Health and Purity	1	2	3	4
Community Support and Unity	1	2	3	4
Divine Strength and Guidance	1	2	3	4

Comparison Evaluation: Growth in Confidence

Instructions:

Now that you've completed both the Pre-Evaluation and Post-Evaluation, use the table below to compare your initial and final confidence levels for each pledge. Reflect

120

on the areas where you've experienced the most growth and consider where you may need further focus.

For guidance, see Appendix F.

To assist you in evaluating your growth throughout the pledges, refer to **Appendix F**, where you will find a detailed **Comparison Evaluation Table**. This table will allow you to compare your initial Pre-Evaluation results with your post-evaluation scores, helping you track your progress and growth as you work through each pledge.

Pledges	Pre-Evaluation Score		Post-Evaluation Score	Change (Growth)
Love and Devotion				
Diligence and Prosperity				
Protection and Love				
Defender of Childhood				
Respect and Honor				
Health and Purity				
Community Support				
Divine Strength and Guidance				

Note:

This evaluation does not comprehensively measure your growth; instead, it offers a rough guideline for reflection, helping you assess areas for improvement and focus. Personal growth is a dynamic process, and the journey continues beyond these measurements.

Creating Your Personalized Certificate

To solidify your pledges, we invite you to create a personalized certificate that will serve as a lasting reminder of your dedication. This certificate is not merely a piece of paper—it represents your commitment to living according to the principles outlined in *The Christian Manhood Pledge.* It symbolizes your reliance on God's strength in every endeavor and your commitment to being a light to those around you."

Scanning the QR code below will direct you to The Manhood Institute website, where you and your accountability partner(s) can enter your names and signatures. This process allows you to formalize your pledge, making your internal commitments a visible testament to your dedication.

What the Certificate Represents

Your certificate will be a tangible expression of the vows you've made:

- A Commitment to God: It signifies your promise to rely on His strength and guidance in every aspect of your life

- A Covenant with Your Accountability Partner(s): It reflects the bond you share with another believer who will walk alongside you, offering support, encouragement, and prayer as you strive to live out these commitments.

- A Testament to Your Faith: Display this certificate as a daily reminder of your chosen path and the man God calls you to be. Let it inspire you to continue growing in faith, serving your community, and honoring God in all you do.

Final Step

HOW TO CREATE YOUR CERTIFICATE

1. Scan the QR Code: Below, you will find a QR code. Scan it with your mobile device to be directed to The Manhood Institute.

2. Enter your details: You and your accountability partner must input your names and signatures.

3. Download and Print: Once you've completed the form, you will receive an 8 1/2 x 11 PDF certificate to print or download. Display this certificate in your home or office as a testament to your commitment.

Moving Forward

As you finalize this vital step, remember that this certificate is not the end but the beginning of a lifelong journey. Have your certificate framed and display it proudly. Keep it where you can see it daily, allowing it to serve as a constant reminder of your promises and the strength you draw from God. Let it inspire and motivate you each day to continue living out the principles of *The Christian Manhood Pledge*, guiding you to honor your commitments with faith, integrity, and perseverance.

May this certificate symbolize the man you are becoming, rooted in faith, empowered by God's strength, and dedicated to His purpose.

As we close this study, I want to leave you with this prayer:

Almighty God,

As we end this journey through **The Christian Manhood Pledge**, we lift our hearts in gratitude for the wisdom and guidance You have provided. Thank You for the insights, the challenges, and the growth that have come from engaging with these principles.

Lord, we ask that You seal the lessons learned deep within our hearts. Empower us to uphold our commitments, living them out with integrity and perseverance daily. May the truths we've discovered transform our thoughts and actions, shaping us into men who reflect Your love and righteousness.

We pray for strength to uphold these pledges, especially in moments of difficulty and temptation. Remind us that we do not walk this path alone but with Your Spirit guiding and empowering us in all we do.

Father, we also lift our accountability partners to You. May our relationships be strengthened through this shared journey. Grant us the humility to seek and give support, the courage to hold each other accountable, and the love to encourage one another in faith.

As we move forward, may the commitments we've made through this study not just be words on a page but a living testimony of our dedication to You. Let our lives reflect the principles of Christian manhood, shining as a light in our families, communities, and beyond.

Thank You, Lord, for Your constant presence and for the work You are doing in our hearts. We trust in Your continued guidance and ask that You bless us as we strive to honor You in all that we do. **In Jesus' name, Amen.**

Peace, Blessing, and Love

APPENDICES

Appendix A

Appendix A: Sample Family Mission Statement - Chapter 3: Protection and Love

The Mauney Family Mission Statement

Our Core Values: Love, Respect, Non-Violence

Love:

We believe love is the foundation of our family. It means unconditionally being there for each other, offering support, understanding, and encouragement. We will show love through actions and words, ensuring everyone feels valued and cherished.

Respect:

Respect is crucial in our family. It means listening to one another, appreciating each other's opinions, and treating everyone with dignity. We will honor each other's differences and seek to understand before being understood.

Non-Violence:

We commit to a non-violent approach in our family in our words and actions. We will resolve conflicts peacefully, using calm communication and empathy. We will strive to create an environment where everyone feels safe to express themselves without fear.

Our Daily Practices:

1. **Communication:** We practice open and honest communication, ensuring everyone's voice is heard. We use 'I' statements to express our feelings and needs without blaming others.

2. **Support:** We will support each other's dreams, goals, and challenges. Whether it's a hug after a tough day or celebrating a success, we are here for each other.

3. **Kindness:** We will choose kindness in our interactions, understanding that our words have power. Even in difficult times, we will speak to each other with love and care.

4. **Conflict Resolution:** We will approach disagreements with an understanding mindset. We will listen to each other's perspectives and work together to find peaceful solutions.

5. **Gratitude:** We will practice gratitude daily, recognizing the blessings we have in each other. We will express our appreciation for one another and our love as a family.

Our Commitment:

We, the Mauney family, commit to living by these values daily. We will remind ourselves of our mission through our actions, words, and the love we show each other. We will display this mission statement in our home as a constant reminder of who we are and what we stand for.

Signed:

[Family Members' Names and Signatures]

Date:

[Date]

Appendix B

Appendix B: Conflict Resolution Role-Play - Chapter 3: Protection and Love

Here's an example of a conflict resolution role-play using "I" statements:

Scenario: John and his sister Sarah have been arguing because John has been borrowing Sarah's car without asking, and Sarah feels disrespected.

Appendices

Role-Play:

John: *"Sarah, I wanted to talk to you about something that's been bothering me. I've noticed that our conversations have been tense lately, and I think it's because of the times I've borrowed your car without asking. I realize now that I should have asked for your permission first."*

Sarah: *"Thank you for bringing it up, John. I appreciate that you're acknowledging this. I have felt frustrated because when you take my car without asking, I feel like my boundaries aren't being respected. I need to know that I can count on having my car when I need it."*

John: *"I understand that, and I'm sorry for making you feel that way. In the future, I'll make sure to ask you before borrowing your car. I don't want you to feel disrespected by my actions."*

Sarah: *"I appreciate that, John. I'm glad we could talk about this without arguing. It's important to me that we respect each other's boundaries, and I'm happy we found a way to resolve this."*

Reflection:

After the role-play, both John and Sarah reflect on how this approach felt compared to past conflicts:

John: *"Using 'I' statements made me feel like I was taking responsibility for my actions without being defensive. It also helped me understand how my actions were affecting Sarah."*

Sarah: *"In the past, I might have reacted with anger or blame, but using 'I' statements helped me express how I felt without escalating the conflict. It felt more productive and respectful."*

This role-play demonstrates how using "I" statements can facilitate a more constructive and nonviolent approach to resolving conflicts.

127

Appendix C

Appendix C: Faith Adventure Map example - Chapter 4: Defender of Childhood

Appendices

Appendix D

Appendix D: Community Mapping Example: Fictitious Community – Oakwood Village Chapter 7: Community Support and Unity

Objective: Identify the needs and strengths of a fictional community, Oakwood Village, and reflect on how to contribute to its development.

Oakwood Village Community Map Overview

Key Locations:

- **Schools**: Oakwood Elementary, Maple Ridge High School
- **Parks**: Greenleaf Park, Oakwood Nature Reserve
- **Local Businesses**: Oakwood Café, Timberline Grocery, Harper's Bookstore
- **Churches and Community Centers**: Oakwood Community Church, Village Activity Center

Community Map Breakdown

Step 1: Create a Map

- The group created a large map of **Oakwood Village** using a poster board. They marked important community landmarks like schools, parks, and businesses.

Step 2: Identify Critical Locations

- **Schools:**
  - *Oakwood Elementary*: This small neighborhood school is known for its close-knit community.
  - *Maple Ridge High School*: Larger school with many extracurricular activities but lacking in funding for certain programs.

- **Parks:**
  - *Greenleaf Park*: A popular hangout spot, but some playground equipment is broken.

129

- *Oakwood Nature Reserve*: Beautiful hiking trails, but litter has been an increasing issue.

- **Local Businesses:**
  - *Oakwood Café*: A family-owned café that hosts local art shows and events.
  - *Timberline Grocery*: The main grocery store with a strong relationship with the community.
  - *Harper's Bookstore*: Known for organizing book clubs and community readings.

- **Churches and Community Centers:**
  - *Oakwood Community Church*: A center for many community activities, food drives, and charity events.
  - *Village Activity Center*: Provides after-school programs and senior fitness classes.

Step 3: Discuss and Mark Needs

- **Maple Ridge High School**: Lacks funding for extracurricular activities like drama and debate teams. Students are missing out on valuable programs.
- **Greenleaf Park**: The playground equipment is broken, posing a safety hazard to children.
- **Oakwood Nature Reserve**: Littering is an issue along hiking trails, diminishing the beauty of the reserve and threatening wildlife.
- **Appendix D (Continue)**
- **Timberline Grocery**: Although essential, they face supply issues, causing prices to increase and affecting lower-income families.

Step 4: Identify and Mark Strengths

- **Oakwood Café**: A hub for community interaction, the café supports local artists and hosts various community events.
- **Harper's Bookstore**: A strong community presence, they organize weekly book readings and provide a space for local authors to showcase their work.
- **Village Activity Center**: Provides vital programs for children, families, and seniors, bringing the community together.

Appendices

Step 5: Reflection and Action After discussing the needs and strengths of **Oakwood Village**, the group identified the following actionable steps:

- **Actionable Focus Area**: Organize a community event to repair the playground equipment in Greenleaf Park. The group will collaborate with the Oakwood Community Church to raise funds for new equipment and recruit volunteers for the project.
- **Long-Term Focus**: Partner with Maple Ridge High School to create a volunteer mentorship program where local professionals offer workshops in arts and debate to compensate for the lack of extracurricular funding.

Example of Oakwood Village Community Map: - Chapter 7: Community Support and Unity

Critical Location	Needs	Strengths
Maple Ridge High School	Lacks funding for extracurricular programs	Strong academic programs
Greenleaf Park	Playground equipment broken	It is a popular hangout spot and a great space for families
Oakwood Nature Reserve	Littering along hiking trails	Beautiful nature trails attract visitors from other areas
Oakwood Café	None	Community hub supports local art and culture
Timberline Grocery	Supply issues causing price hikes	Central to community, excellent customer relations
Harper's Bookstore	None	Organizes community events, supports local authors
Oakwood Community Church	None	Hosts charity events and food drives
Village Activity Center	None	Provides essential programs for children and seniors

131

Appendix E

Appendix E: Example of a "Service Vision Board" - Chapter 7: Community Support and Unity

Appendices

Materials You'll Need:

- Poster board, corkboard, or foam board
- Scissors
- Glue sticks or push pins (if using a corkboard)
- Magazines, printed images, or pictures (related to service, community, etc.)
- Markers or colored pens
- Stickers, ribbons, or any other decorative items
- Inspirational quotes or Bible verses (optional)
- Small notecards or sticky notes (for writing specific goals)

Step-by-Step Instructions:

1. Clarify Your Community Service Goals

- Before creating the vision board, spend some time reflecting on what your community service goals are. Consider the types of service activities you are passionate about (e.g., feeding the homeless, environmental clean-up, tutoring children, etc.).
- Write down a few clear goals you would like to include, such as "Volunteer once a month" or "Organize a community clean-up."

2. Gather Visual Inspiration

- Search through magazines or online for images representing your goals, values, and the community service you want to engage in.
- You might find pictures of people serving, symbols of teamwork, or even images of your community. Look for visuals that inspire you to take action.

3. Find Inspirational Words and Quotes

- Collect quotes or phrases that reflect your motivation for serving others. These could be Bible verses, such as **Matthew 25:40** ("Whatever you did for one of the least of these brothers and sisters of mine, you did for me"), or motivational sayings like "Be the change you want to see in the world."
- Write or print these out to include on your vision board.

4. Organize Your Board Layout

- Divide your board into sections based on the types of community service you plan to engage in. For example, you might have areas for:
  - **Service Projects:** like charity drives, mentorship, or church outreach.
  - **Goals include concrete actions like "volunteering 5 hours a week" or "launching** a new program."
  - **Inspirational Section:** for your quotes, Bible verses, or encouraging words.
  - **Community Focus:** images representing the people or groups you want to help, such as families, schools, or neighborhoods.

5. Arrange and Glue Images and Words

- Please begin placing your images and quotes on the board, arranging them in a meaningful way. Don't worry about being perfect. Let your creativity flow!
- Glue the images down or use push pins to attach them, ensuring they're secure. Leave room for additional photos, words, or decorations as you continue to build your vision over time.

6. Write Down Your Goals

- Use small notecards or sticky notes to write specific, actionable goals for your community service efforts. For instance, "Organize a clothing drive for the shelter in December" or "Join a local food bank by the end of the month."
- Pin or glue these goals in relevant sections of your board.

7. Decorate and Personalize

- Add personal touches like stickers, drawings, or other decorative items to make the vision board uniquely yours. You can include meaningful symbols, such as hearts for compassion or doves for peace.
- Use markers or colored pens to highlight important goals or dates for service events.

8. Display Your Vision Board

- Place your completed community service vision board somewhere you can see it daily, like your office, bedroom, or prayer space. This will remind you of your commitment to serving your community and fulfilling your goals.

Appendices

- As you complete goals or add new ones, update your board regularly.

9. Share It with Your Accountability Partner or Group

- Consider sharing your vision board with a friend, family member, or accountability group for encouragement and support. Having others involved will keep you motivated and help hold you accountable for your community service goals.

Appendix F

Appendix F: Example of Example of Completed Evaluation- Chapter 9

Here is an example of how to fill out the table to reflect on your progress:

Pledges	Pre-Evaluation Score	Post-Evaluation Score	Change (Growth)
Love and Devotion	2	4	+2
Diligence and Prosperity	3	3	0
Protection and Love	1	3	+2
Defender of Childhood	2	4	+2
Honoring and Uplifting Women	3	4	+1
Health and Purity	1	2	+1
Community Support and Unity	2	3	+1
Divine Strength and Guidance	1	4	+3

Explanation:

- **Pre-Evaluation Score**: Enter the score you selected before starting the book (e.g., for "Love and Devotion," you scored 2).
- **Post-Evaluation Score**: After completing the book, enter your new score (e.g., after finishing the book, "Love and Devotion" is now a 4).
- **Change (Growth)**: Subtract your Pre-Evaluation score from your Post-Evaluation score (e.g., 4 - 2 = +2 for "Love and Devotion").

Using this approach will help you see

- **Growth areas**: The pledges where you've improved significantly (e.g., "Divine Strength and Guidance" with a +3 growth).

- **Areas for further focus**: Pledges where there was little or no growth (e.g., "Diligence and Prosperity" with 0 growth).

ABOUT THE AUTHOR

Michael Mauney is the founder and Senior Servant of **The Manhood Institute**. He is also an associate pastor of the Carolina Missionary Baptist Church, Fort Washington, Maryland.

The Manhood Institute is an educational ministry that supports and provides resources to faith-based organizations and community organizations by giving spiritual development and lifestyle development training. Michael Mauney believes that we must make a paradigm shift from traditional ministry to a twenty-first-century ministry that will "Meet people Where They Are and Then Bring Them Where They Need to Be in Relationship to God."

Michael Mauney is a graduate of Shelby High School, Shelby, NC. He received his Bachelor of Science in Computer Science from North Carolina A&T University. He earned his Master of Divinity Degree and his Doctor of Ministry Degree from the Samuel DeWitt Proctor School of Theology of Virginia Union University.

Michael Mauney is a Kappa Alpha Psi Fraternity Inc. member and several other organizations/community affiliations. He contributes to the community and spreads the Gospel of Jesus Christ. He is the proud father of two sons, Caleb and Donovan, who reside with him in Fairfax, Virginia.

EMPOWERING THROUGH EDUCATION AND TRAINING

Introduction: As part of my commitment to the mission of *The Christian Manhood Pledge*, I understand that transformation often begins with education and intentional effort. To this end, I have developed classes, workshops, and lesson plans designed to equip men with the tools they need to grow spiritually, emotionally, and practically.

What I Offer:

1. **Classes and Workshops:**

- Topics Include:
    - Living with Integrity in All Aspects of Life
    - Strengthening Family Relationships
    - Honoring Women and Building Respectful Cultures
    - Stewardship and Financial Empowerment
    - Community Leadership and Service
    - These sessions actively engage participants through hands-on learning opportunities designed to inspire action.

2. **Customized Lesson Plans:**

- Lesson plans tailored for:
    - Churches
    - Men's groups

- Community organizations
- Small group studies

- Each plan is aligned with the principles of *The Christian Manhood Pledge* and includes clear objectives, discussion prompts, and action steps.

3. **Online and In-Person Options:**

- Whether you're looking for virtual lessons or in-person workshops, these offerings are flexible and designed to meet the unique needs of your group.

Why Education Matters:

Knowledge is the foundation of lasting change. I aim to create spaces where men can come together, learn from one another, and take actionable steps toward becoming the individuals God has called them to be.

How to Get Involved:

Suppose you are interested in scheduling a class, hosting a workshop, or using the lesson plans in your community. In that case, I encourage you to reach out. We can make a meaningful impact by equipping men to live with purpose, integrity, and faith.

For inquiries, contact me at:
Email: contact@themanhoodinstitute.com
Website: www.themanhoodinstitute.com

THE JOURNEY TO CHRISTIAN MANHOOD: A PLEDGE FOR BOYS AND YOUNG MEN

COMING SOON!

Prepare to embark on a life-changing path that equips boys and young men with faith, integrity, and purpose.

- Scan the QR Code to join our mailing list and stay connected.
- Email us at contact@themanhoodinstitute.com for inquiries or to express interest.
- Visit our website at themanhoodinstitute.com/books for updates and more details.

The journey starts here—be among the first boys and young men to take the pledge and begin your transformation to Christian Manhood!!